Tasks for Independent Language Learning

David Gardner and
Lindsay Miller, Editors

Teachers of English to Speakers of Other Languages, Inc.

Typeset in Korinna Bold, Berkeley, and Stone Sans
by Capitol Communication Systems, Inc., Crofton, Maryland USA
and printed by
Pantagraph Printing, Bloomington, Illinois USA

Teachers of English to Speakers of Other Languages, Inc.
1600 Cameron Street, Suite 300
Alexandria, VA 22314 USA
Tel 703-836-0774 • Fax 703-836-7864
Director of Communications and Marketing: Helen Kornblum
Senior Editor: Marilyn Kupetz
Copy Editor: Ellen Garshick
Cover Design: Ann Kammerer

ISBN 0-939791-65-X
Library of Congress Catalogue No. 96-060327

TESOL thanks Kathy Trump, the staff, and the students at George Mason University, Fairfax,
Virginia, for their participation and assistance. TESOL also appreciates the cooperation of
Mary Nell Bryant, the staff, and the students of the Adult Learning Center, Alexandria,
Virginia.

CONTENTS

CHAPTER 5: Speaking

CHAPTER 6: Vocabulary

CHAPTER 7: Grammar

CHAPTER 8: Paralinguistics

CHAPTER 9: Self-Assessment

ACKNOWLEDGMENTS

We would like to thank the contributors to this volume, who have taken the time to share with their colleagues ideas for implementing independent language learning. We would also like to thank Marilyn Kupetz, Senior Editor, TESOL Central Office, for her help and Ellen F. Garshick for her speed and efficiency in bringing this volume to press.

The concept of independent language learning is not new. For a long time teachers have been encouraging learners to become more independent in their approach to language learning. Trends in language teaching and research into learning strategies since the early 1970s have enhanced this effort. However, language teaching still remains firmly rooted in the classroom, with the teacher using a set textbook and controlling what is learned, when it is learned, and how it is learned. Breaking away from this pattern has been difficult because of the lack of suitable learning materials. This book gives teachers ideas for developing materials that give their learners more control over their language learning and lead them toward becoming autonomous language learners.

AUTONOMOUS LEARNERS AND INDEPENDENT LANGUAGE LEARNING

Autonomous language learners initiate the planning and implementation of their own learning program. They have specific targets and goals that they set for themselves, and they achieve these goals by making use of opportunities both in and out of the classroom. Independent language learning, a stage between teacher-dependent learning and autonomous learning, is fostered by teacher-developed tasks that encourage learners to start taking responsibility for their learning. As learners become autonomous, they make more decisions for themselves, including whether or not to use the tasks developed by the teacher.

Independent learning tasks can take place in the classroom, outside the classroom, or in a self-access center—a dedicated facility with a materials bank for independent language study. In such a facility, learners can choose to work on their language skills with little or no help from the center staff. Usually, the materials are organized so that they are easily accessible to the learner. Self-access centers can be developed for specific groups of learners, such as engineering students at a university, banking personnel, teacher trainees, or general learners at differing levels of language ability. The type of learners using the facility will determine the types of materials that go into the center.

AIMS OF THIS BOOK

This is an "ideas" book of recipes for independent language learning tasks written for teachers by teachers from secondary and tertiary institutions in the United States, the Pacific Rim, and Europe. The tasks serve as guidelines you can use to create many different activities for your own learners and to set up ways for learners to take control of their learning by deciding how they will complete the task, monitoring how well they perform, and deciding what to do next. It is your job to develop these ideas into creative tasks to promote independent learning. Once you begin to explore ways of setting up the tasks, you will be surprised at the richness of the resulting language learning.

THE LEARNING TASKS

The book contains tasks to suit all types of learners from beginner to advanced and from learners of general English to learners of English for specific purposes. The tasks make use of a variety of resources:

- newspapers and magazines
- simplified readers and novels
- learners' own writing
- computer programs
- native speakers (in the streets, on TV)
- textbooks and course books
- video- and audiotapes
- TV and radio
- songs
- electronic dictionaries

- reference books
- questionnaires and interviews

Most tasks consist of two parts: (a) an explanation of the task and (b) sample worksheets. The explanation contains the following information:

- the learning environment: what level the task is most suitable for; whether learners do the task individually, in pairs, in groups, or with a tutor; and where learners do the task—in class, out of class, or in a self-access center
- the aims, task time, preparation time, and resources needed to do the task
- *Preamble*: the rationale for the task and how it encourages independent learning
- *What the Teacher Has to Do*: step-by-step instructions for setting up the task
- *Learner Preparation*: any necessary pretraining or sensitization
- *Variations*: different ways of doing the task

The accompanying sample worksheets vary. Many contain sections like the following:

- *Before You Begin* prepares learners for the task.
- *The Task* sometimes consists of one activity and sometimes is broken into stages.
- *Self-Assessment* helps learners judge how well they performed on the task.
- *Further Suggestions* help learners take their learning a stage further after completing the task.

ADAPTING THE TASKS TO SUIT YOUR LEARNERS

We have purposely not tried to strictly impose a style on the worksheets in order to demonstrate different ways of setting up independent language learning tasks. You will want to change the content of the worksheets to make them appropriate for your learners. You may also want to vary the degree of user friendliness. For example, you can decide whether to teach your learners the metalanguage of *self-assessment* and *learner training* or to ask them "how well did you do?" and offer them "a few things to think about."

All the learning tasks described in this book have been tried and tested by the contributors. The tasks cover a variety of language learning levels and learning situations: Some are intended to be used with beginners, and others, with more advanced learners. Some are intended for use in a classroom, with a teacher present, whereas others can be used independently in a self-access center. With imagination, however, you can adapt a beginners' task for a more advanced class or present an advanced learners' task in a form to suit a lower level class. Equally, you can adapt the tasks to allow a greater or lesser degree of independence.

The language used throughout this book for describing the tasks and in the worksheets is English. In some situations, however, you may wish to present the instructions in the learners' first language, especially in situations where the learners all speak the same language, or you may wish to keep the instructional language in English but revise it to match the language level of your specific group of learners. Some of the worksheets may need no adaptation for your learners. These decisions are some of those you, as a teacher, must make in preparing a worksheet to promote independent language learning.

A last step in adapting the materials is to catalogue them according to your self-access system.

A WORD OF CAUTION

Learners sometimes need to be persuaded that they can take responsibility for their own language learning. For this reason we have placed the Learner Training chapter at the front of this book. Merely preparing a worksheet for your learners will not make them into independent learners; some preparation, from in-class discussion to full learner-training programs, is necessary. You know your learners best, so you know best how to lead them to independent learning. The success of the ideas in this book depends on the ways in which you implement them.

CHAPTER 1

Learner Training

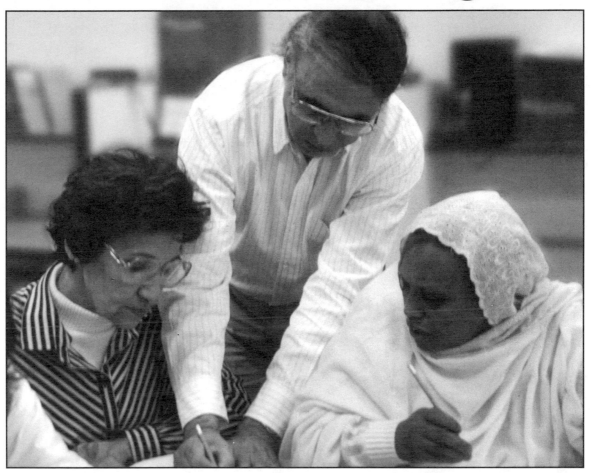

The tasks in this chapter help learners understand their role in learning a language: defining what sort of learners they are, setting priorities for their learning, reflecting on what they have achieved, and dealing with cultural aspects of their language learning.

What's My Style?

☐ beginner
☐ low intermediate
☑ intermediate
☐ advanced

☑ individual
☑ pair
☑ group
☐ tutor-assisted

☑ in class
☑ out of class
☑ self-access center

Aims: Think about the ways one learns best

Task Time: 30 minutes

Preparation Time: 10 minutes

Resources: Worksheet

PREAMBLE

This task helps learners identify those activities, modes of learning, and other aspects of learning that they like best.

WHAT THE TEACHER HAS TO DO

Adapt the worksheet to suit the needs of your learners.

VARIATIONS

1. Have learners work in groups and talk about how they like to learn best.
2. Have learners use the worksheet to survey other learners in order to find out their learning strategy preferences.

CONTRIBUTOR: David Nunan is Director of the English Center and Professor of Applied Linguistics at the University of Hong Kong.

WORKSHEET

This worksheet will help you identify the types of learning activities and modes of learning that you like best.*

BEFORE YOU BEGIN

Think about the language learning experiences and opportunities you have
- in class
- out of class (including self-access learning)

1. Which ways of learning seem to work best for you?
2. Which ways do not seem to work?

*Adapted from *Teaching How to Learn* (pp. 22–23), by K. Willing, 1989, Sydney, Australia: National Center for English Language Teaching and Research.

ACTIVITY 1: HOW DO YOU LIKE TO LEARN?

For each of the following types score yourself 0, 1, 2, or 3 in the brackets to show how you like to learn best.

| 0 = no | 1 = occasionally | 2= usually | 3 = yes |

Type 1

I like to learn by watching and listening to native speakers. [ ]

I like to learn by talking to friends in English. [ ]

At home, I like to learn by watching TV and/or videotapes in English. [ ]

I like to learn by using English out of class. [ ]

I like to learn English words by hearing them. · [ ]

I like to learn by having conversations. [ ]

TOTAL [ ]

Type 2

I like the teacher to explain everything to us. [ ]

I want to write everything in my notebook. [ ]

I like to have my own textbook. [ ]

In class, I like to learn by reading. [ ]

I like to study grammar. [ ]

I like to learn English words by seeing them. [ ]

TOTAL [ ]

Type 3

In class, I like to learn by playing games. [ ]

In class, I like to learn by looking at pictures, films, and videotapes. [ ]

I like to learn English by talking in pairs. [ ]

At home, I like to learn by using audiotapes. [ ]

In class, I like to listen to and use audiotapes. [ ]

I like to go out with the class and practice English. [ ]

TOTAL [ ]

Type 4

I like to study grammar. [ ]

At home, I like to learn by studying English books. [ ]

I like to study English by myself (alone). [ ]

I like the teacher to let me find my mistakes. [ ]

I like the teacher to give us problems to work on. [ ]

At home, I like to learn by reading newspapers. [ ]

TOTAL [ ]

Add up your score for each section and put the number in the *Total* box. The highest total shows what kind of learner you are.

Look at the descriptions below:

Type 1: If you have a high score in this section, you are probably a good communicator. You enjoy interacting with people and using the English you have learned in a natural way.

Type 2: If you have a high score in this section, you probably enjoy learning English in class. You like the teacher to lead you through learning the language.

Type 3: If you have a high score in this section, you probably enjoy learning English by examples. You like learning with other people and you see learning a language as fun.

Type 4: If you have a high score in this section, you probably like learning English by studying it in detail. You like to work by yourself and find out how to use the language on your own.

You may find that you do not fit neatly into any one of the above categories. If so, write out the statements that are most true for you, then try to write a description of yourself as a language learner.

ACTIVITY 2

- Look at the items you have scored with 0. Can you explain why you do not like doing these activities?
- What do you do in place of these activities? Discuss your thoughts with a partner, other group members, or your teacher.

Make the Most of Your Language Learning

☑	beginner
☑	low intermediate
☑	intermediate
☑	advanced
☑	individual
☐	pair
☐	group
☐	tutor-assisted
☐	in class
☐	out of class
☑	self-access center

Aims: Organize learning to achieve realistic goals

Task Time: 15 minutes

Preparation Time: 5 minutes

Resources: Worksheet

PREAMBLE

People embarking on self-access language learning need encouragement and advice as well as learning materials. This task gives advice and encourages learners to identify their most effective learning strategies.

WHAT THE TEACHER HAS TO DO

Adapt the worksheet to suit the needs of your learners.

CONTRIBUTOR: Lucila Makin is a Language Adviser in the Language Center of the University of Cambridge, in the United Kingdom.

WORKSHEET

Before you embark on learning a language, remember that you are busy and already have a lot of work on your hands. But ...

- Life is going to get much busier and more complicated the minute you stop studying and start working.
- During your working life, you will have to do some kind of retraining, which is very likely going to be by distance learning and self-direction, and you will have to juggle it with your work and family commitments.
- It is unlikely that you will again have such easy access to so many facilities for learning a language, so make the most of them.

Now that you are starting, you must have

FAITH

It is possible to learn any language if you put the effort into it. You have already achieved a lot, so you can do it.

List some things that you have already been successful at:

1.

2.

3.

Learner Training

MOTIVATION

You need or want to learn this language. Make the right choice and imagine yourself performing the tasks you want to do when you already know the language.

List some of the things you want to be able to do:

AWARENESS

Observe your working patterns. What are your best times for language learning? (Tick below.)

☐ First thing in the morning (and get it over and done with)

☐ During a break in the middle of the day

☐ Last thing in the evening

TIME

Put aside a realistic amount of time. You are more likely to have five slots of half an hour than one slot of 2½ hours in one go (if you have it, you will use it for your main work). It is better to work for short periods every day, or every other day, than for a long session once a week. From day to day, you will remember what you have learned more easily, and this will give you a greater sense of achievement. Set aside an ideal amount of time and a minimum amount for a busy week.

When are you going to study?

How much time will you spend per week?

- Ideal amount of time:

- Minimum amount of time:

GOALS

Set realistic goals for yourself. Bear in mind your present commitments and the time available, but also take into account the level of proficiency needed for the task you want to carry out in the future. It might be easier to set yourself a goal for today or tomorrow, one for the end of the week, and another for the end of the month.

Time	Goals
Today	
End of the week	
End of the month	

DETERMINATION

After you have decided on a timetable, stick to it for a reasonable length of time. After 2 weeks, you cannot leave it for when you have more time. You will have more time only after retirement, and chances are you will need the language before you retire.

SUPPORT

It might help you to share the experience with another learner. You can study together, practice speaking, compare strategies, measure progress, give each other support, discuss problems, and so on. It can keep you going, especially when the going gets more difficult due to other pressures of work.

Do you know someone to study with? Who?

If not, how could you find a study partner?

ENJOYMENT

You have to like what you are doing. If you find it hard going, try another type of material either for revision, to complement your work, or for the sake of variety. You might discover a new perspective to your learning.

RECORDS

Make notes of the work you do, with as much detail as possible. Whenever necessary, you can refer to them to see what ground you have covered and in what areas you need more practice. It is also rewarding to see how much you have achieved.

FURTHER SUGGESTIONS

1. Always write down thoughts and intentions.
2. Go back to your notes every 15 days to check direction and achievements.

Planning Your Learning

☐ beginner
☐ low intermediate
☑ intermediate
☑ advanced

☑ individual
☐ pair
☐ group
☐ tutor-assisted

☑ in class
☑ out of class
☑ self-access center

Aims: Make realistic study plans by becoming aware of one's limitations

Task Time: 30 minutes

Preparation Time: 10 minutes

Resources: Worksheet

PREAMBLE

Many self-access learners encounter problems because they fail to realize the limitations of their time management skills and learning style. This task makes learners aware of these limitations so that they will not make impossible plans.

WHAT THE TEACHER HAS TO DO

Adapt the worksheet to suit the needs of your learners.

CONTRIBUTOR: Mabel C. P. Wong is a freelance ESL specialist in Victoria, Australia.

WORKSHEET

Before you design a study plan that helps you achieve your personal objectives, you need to think about how much time you have and what your own learning style is. Consider the following:

1. What is your language goal this time?

2. How much time (hours, days, weeks) do you envisage this goal will take?

3. How frequently will you be able to visit the self-access center to achieve your goal, and how much time can you spend during each visit?

4. How long will your study plan last?

5. What kind(s) of activities will you do to achieve your goal?

6. Are you familiar with the equipment and resources in the self-access center?

7. Do you explore new ways to make your learning more interesting and effective?

8. Whom can you ask when you have problems with language and studying strategies?

9. Who can help you locate materials and use the equipment?

10. Which of the following learning styles do you prefer?
    - Work on your own, on materials that you have selected
    - Work on your own, with regular guidance from a consultant
    - Work with other learners as a small group
    - Work with a partner

11. List your strengths and weaknesses in using English.

12. How can you make full use of your strengths and overcome your weaknesses?

Answering the above questions must have made you more aware of your study plan. Now write it down and show it to someone (e.g., a friend, a consultant) for advice.

Assessing Your Language Needs

Aims: Become aware of present and future language needs before starting a self-access learning program

Task Time: 30 minutes

Preparation Time: 10 minutes

Resources: Worksheet

PREAMBLE

Using the self-access center is something new to many learners. This task is designed to help learners understand their own needs so that they are more able to formulate suitable study plans.

WHAT THE TEACHER HAS TO DO

Adapt the worksheet to suit the needs of your learners.

CONTRIBUTOR: Mabel C. P. Wong is a freelance ESL specialist in Victoria, Australia.

WORKSHEET

If self-access learning is something new to you and you don't know how to begin, the following questions may give you a starting point.

Think about each question in terms of the present and the future. Write down your answers.

1. What do/will you need English for? (e.g., study, business)

2. How often do/will you use English?

3. What kind of skills do/will you need? (e.g., report writing, oral presentation)

4. Who do/will you use English with? (e.g., friends, tutors, subordinates, superiors)

By analyzing your answers, you should have an idea about why and when you need English and even the kind of English you need most. Check the catalogue provided in the self-access center to see whether you can find materials relevant to your needs.

Prioritizing Language Needs

- [ ] beginner
- [ ] low intermediate
- [x] intermediate
- [x] advanced

- [x] individual
- [ ] pair
- [ ] group
- [ ] tutor-assisted

- [x] in class
- [x] out of class
- [x] self-access center

Aims: Determine what skills to study and what priorities to place on them

Task Time: 30 minutes

Preparation Time: 10 minutes

Resources: Worksheet

PREAMBLE

Some learners have difficulty verbalizing what they want to learn. They usually feel more comfortable when given a variety of language functions in the form of a checklist. No list can be exhaustive or perfect, however. Some learners might not be able to find skills they actually need and will find consultants' advice useful.

WHAT THE TEACHER HAS TO DO

Adapt the worksheet to suit the needs of your learners.

CONTRIBUTOR: Mabel C. P. Wong is a freelance ESL specialist in Victoria, Australia.

WORKSHEET

Below are some common language skills. Tick the skill(s) you need most at present or will need in the future. Do not choose too many because it will be more efficient to work consistently on a few areas at a time. Put down a number (1 = very poor; 5 = very good) in the last column to indicate your proficiency in items you have ticked.

Language focus	Needs		Proficiency (1 = very poor; 5 = very good)
	Now	Future	
Reading			
Academic articles or texts			
Literature or readers			
Newspapers and magazines			
Advertisements and public information			
Others:			
Writing			
Academic articles or papers			
Creative writing			
Curriculum vitae and résumés			

Language focus	Needs		Proficiency (1 = very poor; 5 = very good)
	Now	Future	
Descriptions			
A diary			
Essays			
Formal letters			
Forms			
Informal letters			
Instructions/leaflets/brochures			
Memos and messages			
Minutes			
Newspaper articles			
Reports and proposals			
Talks and presentations			
Others:			
Listening			
Business meetings			
Conversations			
Dictations			
Discussions			
Dramas			
Entertainment (e.g., movies)			
Interviews			
Lectures			
TV/radio news			
Songs/music			
Stories			
Talks and presentations			
Telephone conversations			
Others:			
Speaking			
Business meetings			
Social conversations			
Group discussions			
Interviews			
Interactive skills			

Language focus	Needs		Proficiency (1 = very poor; 5 = very good)
	Now	Future	
Role plays and simulations			
Talks and presentations			
Telephone conversations			
Storytelling			
Others:			
Grammar			
Pronunciation			
Vocabulary			
Others			

Now that you have prioritized your needs, you are ready to design a study plan for yourself. The tasks Planning Your Learning (see p. 9) and Learner Contract (see p. 16) can help.

Focusing on Your Language Needs

- [ ] beginner
- [ ] low intermediate
- [✔] intermediate
- [✔] advanced

- [✔] individual
- [ ] pair
- [ ] group
- [ ] tutor-assisted

- [✔] in class
- [✔] out of class
- [✔] self-access center

Aims: Focus on subgoals within overall goals

Task Time: 10 minutes

Preparation Time: 1 minute

Resources: Worksheet

PREAMBLE

Sometimes learners get carried away with all the things they want to do. This very short task helps them focus on very specific subgoals that fall within their overall goals.

WHAT THE TEACHER HAS TO DO

Adapt the worksheet to suit the needs of your learners.

CONTRIBUTOR: Mabel C. P. Wong is a freelance ESL specialist in Victoria, Australia.

WORKSHEET

PREPARATION

It is helpful to do the task Prioritizing Language Needs (see p. 12) before doing this one.

ACTIVITY

1. Think of a language need that you have decided to work on.

2. Break it down into smaller subgoals. For example, subgoals for *reading academic articles* could be *locating main ideas in the text*, *identifying major and minor details*, and *summarizing and note-taking*.

Target Need: _____

Subgoals: 1. _____

2. _____

3. _____

4. _____

Once you know your subgoals, it will be easier to see what you have to do.

FURTHER SUGGESTION

Use this method for each new need that you identify.

Learner Contract

- [ ] beginner
- [ ] low intermediate
- [x] intermediate
- [x] advanced

- [x] individual
- [ ] pair
- [ ] group
- [ ] tutor-assisted

- [x] in class
- [x] out of class
- [x] self-access center

Aims: Commit to study plans and stick to them consistently

Task Time: 30 minutes

Preparation Time: 10 minutes

Resources: Worksheet

PREAMBLE

Learners involved in independent learning activities may lose momentum very quickly, as self-access learning requires a lot of self-control. The learner contract in this task makes learners feel that it is their own responsibility to complete what they have agreed to do.

WHAT THE TEACHER HAS TO DO

Adapt the worksheet to suit the needs of your learners.

CONTRIBUTOR: Mabel C. P. Wong is a freelance ESL specialist in Victoria, Australia.

WORKSHEET

This worksheet will help you commit yourself to a realistic goal. Fill out the contract below and discuss it with a consultant if necessary. Use a contract for only one goal. Remember to make realistic estimates of your time. If you underestimate what you can do, you will achieve very little; if you overestimate, you will probably have a lot of unfinished tasks.

Name: _____

This plan covers the period _____ hours per week/month for the next _____ weeks/months.

Goal: By the end of this period, I want to be able to _____
I am going to achieve my goal by [learning methods] _____
I am going to assess my own achievement by _____
I am going to meet the consultant _____ times a week/a month to talk about my progress.

WORKSHEET

Below is my study plan for this period of time:

Date and time	Subgoal(s)	No. of hours	Activities/materials	Remarks

Signed _____ Consultant _____ Date _____

Finding Self-Access Activities

- [ ] beginner
- [ ] low intermediate
- [✔] intermediate
- [✔] advanced

- [✔] individual
- [✔] pair
- [✔] group
- [ ] tutor-assisted

- [ ] in class
- [✔] out of class
- [✔] self-access center

Aims: Reflect on self-access activities in order to become more autonomous

Task Time: Variable

Preparation Time: 0–10 minutes

Resources: Worksheets 1 and 2

PREAMBLE

The worksheets in this task encourage learners to work on their own, either individually or in groups, by using all the resources available outside the classroom. Worksheet 2 will help them keep a record of their work, which will encourage them to work regularly.

WHAT THE TEACHER HAS TO DO

Adapt the worksheets to suit your learners and the resources available locally.

VARIATION

Adapt the task so that it begins in the classroom and continues as an independent task. In class, invite learners to suggest out-of-class activities that they could undertake independently either as individuals or in groups. In this way everyone in the class hears all the good ideas.

CONTRIBUTOR: Carmen F. Santás is a teacher in the secondary school Antón Fraguas de Fontiñas and a teacher trainer in the Institute of Education of the University of Santiago de Compostela, Spain.

WORKSHEET

WORKSHEET 1

Read this list of things you can do to improve your English without a teacher. As you read, put a tick (✔) by the things you already do and an asterisk (*) by the things you want to do.

Activity	✔ or *
Review work done at school. Do it again on your own to see if you still remember. Keep all work done in class and make sure you correct it properly. Keep a record of your mistakes. Read texts and review exercises several times.	
Borrow English materials: readers, audiotapes, workbooks with answer key, and so on.	
Watch films in English with subtitles in your own language.	

Activity	✔ or *
Watch films in English with subtitles in English. (Ask your teacher; these films are designed for deaf people but are useful for improving your English.)	
Listen to music in English and try to understand the lyrics. Prepare an activity based on it to do in class.	
Read books, either in the original version or in simplified readers. Remember that some readers come with an audiotape you can listen to.	
Read newspapers or magazines in English.	
Talk to native speakers, such as tourists, whenever you can.	
Watch English programs on TV.	
Do exercises and activities with an answer key. There are lots of them. Look in the library or let your teacher know what you would like.	
Whenever you can afford it, go to a good bookshop and look at the English language section. Some of the many interesting materials are famous stories with audiotapes, videotapes with sing-along songs, simplified readers, comics, magazines, and computer games. Don't forget to share what you find with your classmates.	
Find friends and classmates who want to do the same activities as you. You might want to work alone on some. Use Worksheet 2 to keep a record of what you do.	

WORKSHEET

WORKSHEET 2

- Make a record sheet like the example below. Use it to record what you have done.
- Keep everything you do in a folder.
- You can do things in groups, but each of you must keep a record of your own work.

What I have done	What I learned	How I learned it	Date and time spent
Example: *I have listened to ..., talked/read, written ....*	**Example:** *I learned new words related to .... I also learned some expressions like .... I reviewed tenses and .... enlarged my cultural knowledge about ....*	First I .... Then .... Finally .... **Example:** *Made mind maps with the vocabulary, wrote examples of new verbs, and worked out the rule/ checked a grammar resource. Made a list with useful expressions. Listened once for general meaning and a second time for specific information to do the task. Designed an activity and tried to do it myself and then I could correct my own mistakes. Took notes as I read. I rewrote something I was not satisfied with.*	**Example:** *11th October About 2 hours*

Learner Training

Watching TV

Aims: Become a proactive and reflective learner of listening skills

Task Time: Variable

Preparation Time: 5 minutes

Resources: Videotaped documentaries, comedies, news programs, or other programs; worksheet

PREAMBLE

This task uses TV watching to make learners aware of how they learn. It is a summing-up activity.

WHAT THE TEACHER HAS TO DO

1. Adapt the worksheet to suit your learners' needs.
2. Make the worksheet available near videotapes and general listening materials.

LEARNER PREPARATION

Give some guidance in setting and understanding listening objectives.

CONTRIBUTOR: José Lai is a Senior Language Instructor in the English Language Teaching Unit of the Chinese University of Hong Kong.

WORKSHEET

The aim of this worksheet is to make you aware of the way you learn. You can use it with any videotape (in the self-access center or at home). You can use it alone or with one or more friends and discuss your ideas afterwards.

PREPARATION

1. Select a videotape that interests you.
2. Set your own listening objectives (i.e., decide why you are watching the videotape).

ACTIVITY

Take notes on the following points while you are watching the videotape.

1. What do you do to achieve your listening objective?
2. Describe the major difficulties you have and the respective listening strategies and skills you employ to help understand the program. Illustrate them with concrete examples from the program.
3. Write about your reaction to the program: Did you like it? Would you recommend it? Was it good as a listening exercise? Was it difficult for you to understand? Why or why not?
4. Give suggestions for how learners can best use programs like this to improve listening skills.

Cultural Awareness Training

☐ beginner
☐ low intermediate
☑ intermediate
☑ advanced

☐ individual
☐ pair
☑ group
☐ tutor-assisted

☑ in class
☐ out of class
☐ self-access center

Aims: Celebrate the richness of one's own culture by teaching classmates and the teacher about it

Task Time: 1–2 hours

Preparation Time: 10–15 minutes

Resources: Worksheet

PREAMBLE

This task shows learners that every culture is unique and makes them aware of the many diverse cultures within the world.

WHAT THE TEACHER HAS TO DO

1. Prepare a worksheet similar to the one below.
2. Group the learners by common language (e.g., all Korean speakers) if feasible; otherwise, separate them by gender. Each group should have two to three learners.
3. Distribute the worksheets and ask the learners to spend a few minutes discussing each topic.
4. After 20–25 minutes, ask the learners to change groups and share their ideas with each other.
5. Hold a class discussion about cultural awareness and sensitivity training.

LEARNER PREPARATION

Ask your learners to think about and collect examples of what makes their culture different from the local one.

VARIATION

As a winding-up activity, have the class vote on the five most important points to keep in mind when traveling outside the local culture (e.g., always take your shoes off when entering a house; learn to use chopsticks).

CONTRIBUTOR: Dennis Bricault is Director of ESL Programs and Instructor in Spanish at North Park College, Chicago, Illinois, in the United States.

WORKSHEET

ACTIVITY

Work with a partner or in groups with learners from your own cultural background. Discuss the topics below and describe what makes your culture special. Remember, you are not comparing cultures; you are describing your culture.

- Nonverbal communication (gestures, facial expressions)

- Names: meanings, nicknames

- Holidays

- Music and the arts

- Religion

- Your native language: grammar, pronunciation, features that your teacher should know about

- Meeting, greeting, and saying good-bye

- Attitudes: time and punctuality

- Attitudes: family and friends

- Attitudes: showing emotions

- Attitudes: work and study

- Attitudes: men and women

- Food and eating

- Taboo gestures and topics: things you shouldn't talk about or do in your country

- Homes and living space: the typical home in your country

- Impolite behavior: things that people in your country find offensive

- Difficulties that students from your country have with English

Once you have finished your discussion, change groups and discuss your ideas about your own culture with learners from other cultures. End your discussion by talking about some of the difficulties in learning English that are common to people from your country.

FURTHER SUGGESTION

Use the information you have been collecting to write an essay about your country or for a project on your country.

CHAPTER 2

Reading

This section offers a variety of exercises that help learners become more independent readers. The tasks cover extensive and intensive reading, thinking about different styles of texts, using nontext clues such as pictures to understand a text better, and modeling pronunciation and intonation patterns with the help of a written text. Throughout the tasks learners are asked to stop and think about how they read and what strategies they use most effectively.

Newspaper and Magazine "Issues"

☐ beginner
☐ low intermediate
✔ intermediate
✔ advanced

✔ individual
✔ pair
✔ group
☐ tutor-assisted

✔ in class
✔ out of class
✔ self-access center

Aims: Explore current provocative issues in the media; focus on the main points of an article and analyze personal reactions to it

Task Time: 30–45 minutes (depending on the length of the article)

Preparation Time: 15 minutes

Resources: Media articles from newspapers or magazines, worksheet, answer key

PREAMBLE

This task helps learners extract the main points from a written text. It also helps them relate the issue covered in the text to their lives as both individuals and members of their societies. Learners first read for the gist of the article and then apply this knowledge in a larger social context. By using focus questions and phrases, learners can explore fairly complex issues and offer personal reactions and suggestions.

WHAT THE TEACHER HAS TO DO

1. Select an interesting article from a current newspaper or magazine.
2. Adapt the worksheet to suit the needs of your learners.
3. Prepare an answer key containing suggested answers for Steps 1 and 2 of the activity.

VARIATIONS

1. Have the learners collect a large number of articles and create "media folders."
2. Have the learners follow an ongoing story and record the development of events as a progressive story line.
3. Have the learners identify vocabulary items from various articles and create vocabulary keys.
4. To use the task with groups, have learners complete the worksheets individually then meet in small groups to discuss further the issues raised. Then ask them to compare their written responses and discuss their various similarities and differences with their peers.

CONTRIBUTOR: Elsie Christopher is an Instructor in the Language Center of Hong Kong University of Science and Technology.

WORKSHEET

The purpose of this worksheet is to help you understand the issues discussed in a newspaper or magazine article and to use what you find out in a wider context.

PREPARATION

Make sure you have the following newspaper or magazine article:

Title of the article: _____

Catalogue No.: _____

ACTIVITY

1. List the main points in the article.

2. Write answers to these questions:

    a. Is the article only relevant to one place, or can it be related to other issues in other parts of the world?

    b. Is the issue discussed in the article a personal one, or can it be related to the whole of society? Note the reasons for your answer.

    c. Did you discover any points in the article that were confusing or difficult to understand? List them.

3. Write down what you feel and think about the issues discussed in the article. Notice the difference between sentences like

    I feel sad about ... because ....

    and

    I think the problem is caused by ... because ....

4. Make any suggestions that you think are relevant to the issues discussed (e.g., *I would like to suggest ....*).

VOCABULARY

List any new words that you found when reading the article. Check the words in a dictionary.

FURTHER SUGGESTIONS

Find a partner or a small group of friends and discuss the issues raised in the article you have read. Compare your thoughts and feelings with those of the other people. Then compare the suggestions you made.

Text Review

- [ ] beginner
- [ ] low intermediate
- [x] intermediate
- [ ] advanced

- [x] individual
- [x] pair
- [ ] group
- [ ] tutor-assisted

- [x] in class
- [x] out of class
- [x] self-access center

Aims: Think about different writing styles; review a reading text

Task Time: 45 minutes

Preparation Time: 20 minutes

Resources: Piece of writing taken from a magazine, newspaper, advertisement, novel, or other source; worksheet; answer key

PREAMBLE

This task helps learners recognize that there are different writing styles and that we read different kinds of text in different ways. For example, an advertisement is not read in the same way as a magazine article. Learners also practice summarizing their views on a text.

WHAT THE TEACHER HAS TO DO

1. Select a piece of writing taken from a magazine, newspaper, advertisement, novel, or other source.
2. Adapt the worksheet to the type of writing being used.
3. Complete an answer key for the piece of writing selected.

LEARNER PREPARATION

Encourage learners to think about or discuss in groups the kind of materials they read on a daily basis. These could include anything from bus timetables to billboard advertisements.

VARIATIONS

1. Build up a collection of learner reviews of readers and other texts available in the self-access center. Have learners using this worksheet compare their review with earlier ones.
2. Adapt the worksheet for reviews of TV programs, films, and videotapes.
3. To use the task with pairs, have the learners complete the worksheet independently then discuss their answers with a partner.

CONTRIBUTOR: Sue Fitzgerald is an Instructor at the English Language Study-Center of Hong Kong Polytechnic University.

WORKSHEET

PREPARATION

For this worksheet you need Magazine Text No. _____.

BEFORE YOU BEGIN

Think about what you like and dislike about reading magazines.

WORKSHEET

ACTIVITY

Complete the following boxes:

Title of article:

Category (e.g., news, story):

Expected audience:

Purpose of article:

I found the article interesting because:

I didn't like the article because:

FURTHER SUGGESTIONS

1. Use the above criteria to review other texts you read, films you watch, or programs on TV.
2. Do a survey of the reading likes and dislikes of other learners. Use the worksheet as a questionnaire or as a set of questions for an interview.

Surveying a Text for General Information

Aims: Survey a text and predict its content before reading it in detail

Task Time: 25 minutes

Preparation Time: 20 minutes

Resources: Text or article that has pictures and captions, worksheet, answer key

PREAMBLE

This task shows learners that in reading a text it is more effective to get the general idea before going into its details, and surveying is one strategy to use in order to find the general idea. After surveying, learners can decide whether the text is of interest to them and whether to continue reading or not.

WHAT THE TEACHER HAS TO DO

1. Select a text from a newspaper, magazine, journal, textbook, or another source that is suitable for your learners. The general content of the text should be familiar to them.
2. Make two copies of the text. Label one *Version A* and the other *Version B*.
3. Adapt Version A by blanking out everything *except* the title, the pictures (with captions), the introductory paragraph, and the first sentence of the remaining paragraphs. Leave Version B complete.
4. Attach both texts to the worksheet.
5. Prepare an explanation of what the text is about and add it to the answer key.

CONTRIBUTOR: Sonthida Keyuravong is a Senior Language Instructor in the English Department at Chiang Mai University, Thailand.

WORKSHEET

PREPARATION

Make sure you have Version A and Version B of the following text: _____

BEFORE YOU BEGIN

Think about your way of reading and choose one of the following answers to this question: What do you do if you want to know roughly what a text is about in a few minutes?

1. Read the title.
2. Read the title and read the text in detail very quickly.
3. Read the title, look at the pictures and caption, read the first paragraph, and read the first sentence of each paragraph very quickly.

Do *not* check your answer yet.

ACTIVITY 1

Look at Version A of the text and write down what you think it is about. Do *not* check your answers yet.

ACTIVITY 2

Read Version B, which is the full text. Check to see if you have made the right guesses in Activity 1. If you think you have not guessed well, change your answers.

ASSESSMENT

Check your answers against the answer key. Are you satisfied with your performance? If not, what are you going to do?

TASK EVALUATION

Think about the following questions:

1. Has this worksheet helped you?
2. Is surveying a useful strategy to use before you read a text in detail?
3. Will you use this strategy when reading?

FURTHER SUGGESTION

Practice surveying by yourself by looking at the titles or headings of a text and predicting what it is about before you read it. Then read the text to see whether you are right.

ANSWER KEY

What do you do if you want to know roughly what a text is about in a few minutes?

Answer 3 is the best answer. This strategy is used to find out the general idea of the text. You will then know whether you want to continue reading or not.

Activities 1 and 2: What the Text Is About

[Add an explanation of the text here.]

It is all right if you have made wrong predictions. Practice will help you make more accurate predictions in the future.

Recognizing the Meaning of Connectors

Aims: Recognize the meaning of connectors when reading a text

Task Time: 30 minutes

Preparation Time: 1 hour

Resources: Texts or articles that have connectors, worksheet, answer key

PREAMBLE

This task helps learners realize the importance of connectors. They are "cues" to rely on in order to get an idea of what kind of sentence is likely to follow.

WHAT THE TEACHER HAS TO DO

1. Write a text containing connectors relevant to your learners.
2. Break the text immediately after each connector.
3. Following the break, supply two or more alternative completions for the sentence. Only one should be acceptable.
4. Prepare an answer key that explains the correct choices.
5. Add to the worksheet and answer key a reference to a grammar book so learners can check on the use of the connectors by themselves when they run into problems.

VARIATION

Make a series of exercises that cover different types of connectors. These might include connectors expressing cause-effect relationships, comparisons, contrasts, and others.

CONTRIBUTOR: Sonthida Keyuravong is a Senior Language Instructor in the English Department at Chiang Mai University, Thailand.

WORKSHEET

ACTIVITY

Read the following text. Each time a sentence is broken, choose a correct ending.

Although oil leaks naturally into the sea from sources beneath the ocean bottom, the quantities produced by this natural leakage are small. Humans, however, ...

1. a. ... are trying to find methods to prevent this natural leakage.

   b. ... are responsible for the dumping of ten times as much oil into the sea.

This is one of the causes of global environmental pollution, but ...

2. a. ... we are slow to acknowledge it.

   b. ... it causes a lot of damage.

[Continue until the end of the text.]

SELF-ASSESSMENT

1. Check your answers against the answer key.
2. Are you satisfied with your performance?

FURTHER SUGGESTIONS

If you have trouble using connectors, check them in the following grammar reference

book: _____

ANSWER KEY

No.	Answer	Explanation
1	b	*However* contrasts small quantities and large quantities.
2	a	*But* contrasts a known cause and lack of acknowledgment of the cause.

If you do not understand the use of some of the connectors in the activity, check the

following grammar reference book: _____

Reading

Understanding
News Stories

- ☑ beginner
- ☑ low intermediate
- ☑ intermediate
- ☐ advanced

- ☑ individual
- ☑ pair
- ☐ group
- ☐ tutor-assisted

- ☐ in class
- ☐ out of class
- ☑ self-access center

Aims: Practice reading news leads

Task Time: 30 minutes

Preparation Time: 25 minutes

Resources: Newspaper stories, worksheet, answer key

PREAMBLE

Newspapers are an important source of authentic language, but they can be difficult to follow. This task helps learners make good use of newspaper articles by showing them how to make use of the visual and linguistic cues they offer.

WHAT THE TEACHER HAS TO DO

1. Look in the newspaper for six news items that have a picture, a headline, and an article. The articles should contain information that falls into the categories of *who*, *what*, *when*, *where*, *why*, and *how*.
2. Adapt the worksheet to suit the needs of your learners. (You might want to change or add to the categories offered.)
3. Number the news items.
4. Attach the six news items to the worksheet. (For durability, mount them on cards, laminate them, or both.)
5. Write an answer key.

VARIATIONS

1. Restrict the task to one particular type of news in order to focus on subject-based vocabulary.
2. Adapt the task for television or radio news by substituting videotape or audiotape recordings for newspaper cuttings.

CONTRIBUTOR: Sonthida Keyuravong is a Senior Language Instructor in the English Department at Chiang Mai University, Thailand.

WORKSHEET

This worksheet is designed to help you
1. Practice picking up clues from pictures and headlines
2. Practice reading for detailed information

For the following activities use the news stories attached to this worksheet.

ACTIVITY 1

Look at the pictures and the headlines *only* for each news story. Classify each by type of news. Use the following types:

a. Disasters
b. Politics
c. Science and technology

d. Entertainment
e. Crime
f. Business

News story	Type of news
No. 1	
No. 2	
No. 3	
No. 4	
No. 5	
No. 6	

ACTIVITY 2

Select any of the news items that interest you and answer as many of the following questions as you can:

1. What happened?
2. Why did it happen?
3. When did it happen?
4. Where did it happen?
5. How did it happen?
6. Who was involved?

CHECK YOUR ANSWERS

Check the answer keys for both activities. The accuracy of your answers in Activity 1 will tell you how good you are at picking up clues from pictures and headlines. The accuracy of your answers in Activity 2 will tell you how good you are at understanding the detail of the stories.

FURTHER SUGGESTION

Find a partner who is interested in doing more exercises like this one. Use an English language newspaper to create exercises and answer keys for each other.

Relevant Replies

Aims: Understand the language of agreeing, warning, and giving advice in context

Task Time: 25 minutes

Preparation Time: 15 minutes

Resources: Newspaper or magazine interview, worksheet, answer key

PREAMBLE

This task prepares learners to read dialogues. It helps them follow the discussion and recognize relevant expressions for agreement, warnings, and advice.

WHAT THE TEACHER HAS TO DO

1. Choose a newspaper or magazine interview or article that contains dialogue between two or more people.
2. Add line numbers to the dialogue.
3. Adapt the worksheet to suit the needs of your learners.
4. Prepare an answer key to go with the worksheet.

LEARNER PREPARATION

Encourage the learners to use dictionaries.

VARIATIONS

1. To use this task with beginners or low intermediate learners, replace the newspaper or magazine interview with one you write yourself. It should consist mostly of grammatical structures and vocabulary with which the learners are familiar.
2. Use the task as a listening activity by replacing the newspaper or magazine interview with a video- or audiotaped interview.
3. To use the task for pair or group work, ask learners to find articles and make answer keys. Then have the learners exchange their articles and answer keys to do the task. If there are any disagreements, tell the learners to seek help initially from a dictionary and ultimately from a teacher. Collect these extra articles with their answer keys. Check them and use them as a materials bank for future learners.

CONTRIBUTORS: Paul Kovács and Steve Corfield are EFL teachers at International House in Huelva, Spain.

WORKSHEET

PREPARATION

You need the following newspaper or magazine article:

Catalogue No.: _____

Article title: _____

WORKSHEET

BEFORE YOU BEGIN

1. Think of ways to do the following in English:
   a. Agree or disagree
   b. Warn
   c. Give advice

ACTIVITY

As you read the article, look for phrases that agree, disagree, warn, or give advice. Write them in the table below and add the meaning. The first one is done as an example.

Line no.	Phrase	Meaning (agree, disagree, warn, give advice)
3	*I'd accept it if I were you.*	*Give advice*

When you have finished, check your answers against the answer key.

FURTHER SUGGESTIONS

Find someone you can have a conversation with in English (e.g., a classmate, a tourist, a relative). Use the phrases you have seen here.

Jigsaw Reading

Aims: Use reading to enhance and activate other skills; acquire language through exposure to interactive tasks; read extensively as a communicative, cooperative task

Task Time: 30–50 minutes (depending on the length of the chosen text)

Preparation Time: 20 minutes

Resources: First three pages of a reader, worksheet, answer key

PREAMBLE

This task encourages extensive reading. By working in groups at the beginning of the task, learners can help one another with key vocabulary and structures, which stimulates them to read on. They also make their own group predictions, which gets them more involved. Reading the text more than once but with a specific aim in mind helps them acquire and process the new language unconsciously.

WHAT THE TEACHER HAS TO DO

1. Choose a reader that is appropriate to your learners
2. Photocopy the first three pages and label them A, B, and C respectively. Write 12 questions in the first column of the worksheet. Include 4 questions for each of the three passages, but mix them up. Make copies for each learner. (Note: In some countries it is not permissible to photocopy pages from a book. An alternative would be to take the actual pages from the book and laminate them.)
3. Write an answer key for the questions.

VARIATION

1. Use different kinds of reading texts.
2. Ask the learners to write the next chapters, predicting how the story unfolds.
3. Encourage learners who prefer speaking and acting to improvise a role play of what happens next. After the role play, have them read the rest of the text and compare their version with the original.

CONTRIBUTOR: Carmen F. Santás is a teacher in the secondary school Antón Fraguas de Fontiñas and a teacher trainer in the Institute of Education of the University of Santiago de Compostela, Spain.

WORKSHEET

PREPARATION

For this worksheet you need the following text:

Title: _____

The text is divided into Parts A, B, and C. You will need at least three people to make this task work.

WORKSHEET

INSTRUCTIONS

1. Split up into three groups. Each group should take one part of the text.
2. Read your part. With your group, write questions about the parts that are missing.
3. Make new groups consisting of three people who have each read one of the parts.
4. Without looking at the texts, explain the story and answer each other's questions.
5. Still without looking at the texts, try to write answers to the following questions:
   a. How many people are involved in the story?
   b. What is the relationship between the man and the woman?
   c. Where does the story take place? How do you know?
   d. [Write other questions suitable to the text.]
   e.
   f.
   g.
6. Working together, read all the parts and check and discuss your answers. You can make changes or add to your answers, or completely rewrite them.

HOW WELL DID YOU DO?

When you have finished changing your answers, check them against the answer key.

Shadow Reading

Aims: Listen to and read texts simultaneously

Task Time: 1 hour

Preparation Time: 30 minutes

Resources: Authentic text, audiotape, recorder, worksheet

PREAMBLE

When encountering new words in reading, many learners mentally impose incorrect pronunciations on the words. This task overcomes this problem by providing model pronunciation and intonation during the reading process.

WHAT THE TEACHER HAS TO DO

1. Select a text that is appropriate for the language level you want to focus on. The text can be any length. It should contain words with which the learners will be unfamiliar.
2. Record a spoken version of the text. If you wish to maintain authenticity, enlist the aid of a native speaker to read the text.
3. Adapt the worksheet to meet the needs of your learners.

VARIATIONS

1. Make a series of graded worksheets for shadow reading. Learners can find their own level and gradually move to more difficult texts.
2. To make this a reading-speaking task, provide a blank audiotape along with the recorded version of the text and ask learners to record themselves speaking the text. Then have them listen to both audiotapes and compare their pronunciation with that of the model speaker.

CONTRIBUTOR: Alison Wong is a Lecturer in the Language Institute at the City University of Hong Kong.

WORKSHEET

The purpose of this worksheet is to help you learn new words as you read.

PREPARATION

To use this worksheet you need:

1. Audiotape No. _____

2. Text No. _____

ACTIVITY

1. Listen to the audiotape and read the text at the same time. Do not stop.

2. Now listen and read again. This time, stop whenever you meet a word you are unfamiliar with and do the following:

   a. Listen to the word again.

   b. Write it in the first column of the table below.

   c. Guess what it means by looking at the sentences around it.

   d. Write what you think it means in the second column of the table.

New word	What you think it means	What it really means

3. Look in a dictionary for the meanings of the words and add them to the third column of the table. How good were your guesses?

4. Say the new words to yourself to practice the pronunciation. If you can't remember how to pronounce them, listen to the audiotape again.

FURTHER SUGGESTIONS

If you find this a useful way of learning, ask your teacher to make audiotapes of texts you are interested in.

CHAPTER 3

Writing

The tasks in this chapter cover a number of problem areas for developing writers: examining one's own writing, developing ideas for writing, learning to identify errors, and discovering how different genres affect the written message. Other tasks focus on using a thesaurus, using a computer to improve one's writing, and working on writing in groups.

Opinions and Support

Aims: Review language for agreeing and disagreeing; think creatively about issues; learn about the "letter to the editor" genre of writing and the idea of supporting opinions with evidence

Task Time: 30–60 minutes initially; 15–20 minutes each subsequent time

Preparation Time: 25 minutes

Resources: Sample letter to the editor, responses to the letter, worksheets, answer key

PREAMBLE

Using evidence, examples, or reasons to state an opinion adds depth to an argument, in contrast to stating opinions without support (*I think ...*, *I agree*, *I don't think so*). This task demonstrates and helps learners practice the language for adding support to their opinions.

WHAT THE TEACHER HAS TO DO

1. Select a letter to the editor and one or more responses to that letter from the local newspaper to use as a sample of the genre. Sometimes letters are written in response to articles, so you may want to include the article that inspired the letter as well.
2. Attach your selection to Worksheet 1.
3. Write an answer key for Worksheet 1.
4. Prepare a series of issues for Worksheet 2. Put each issue in a separate folder.

LEARNER PREPARATION

Be sure that learners understand that Worksheet 1 is a receptive activity and that their goal is to become aware of how opinions are supported. Worksheet 2, on the other hand, is a productive activity.

VARIATION

1. To make this a speaking/listening task, replace Worksheet 2 with an audiotape that learners add to.
2. For pairs or groups, have learners use the following procedure:
   - Read Worksheet 1 together and discuss the questions.
   - Circulate Worksheet 2 around the group. (A large group could do this over a number of days.)
   - Meet to discuss the "for" and "against" arguments.

CONTRIBUTORS: Eric Bray teaches English at Doshisha University and Doshisha Women's College in Japan. Kenny Harsch is Director of English Education at Kobe YMCA College and teaches English composition and conversation at Kobe City University of Foreign Studies in Japan.

WORKSHEET 1

Most English newspapers have a section called "Letters to the Editor." In this section, people write their opinions about current issues or local happenings (often in response to articles that recently appeared in the newspaper). Sometimes other readers will send in response letters that agree or disagree with the opinion expressed in the first letter.

In these letters, the writers typically express their opinions and give evidence to support those opinions. The support is a very important part of these letters, because it gives weight to their argument.

Here is a letter to the editor from the newspaper and a response to that letter. Make a note of the opinions and the supporting evidence.

[sample letter here]

Now answer these questions:

1. What language did the writers use to express their opinions? What language did they use to give evidence? Can you see a significant difference?
2. Without the supporting evidence, how strong are the writers' arguments?

WORKSHEET 2

Choose one of the issues in the folders. Read the letters in the folder and decide on your opinion about the issue. Be sure to support your opinion with examples or reasons.

Write your opinion (with support) on the form below. If someone has already written an opinion before you, read it and decide whether you agree or disagree with it.

Issue:

Name	For or against	Opinion

Requests and Reasons

Aims: Review language for making, granting, and denying requests and for making requests accompanied by reasons; have input into what happens in class

Task Time: 20–60 minutes

Preparation Time: None

Resources: Worksheet, answer key

PREAMBLE

Although simple requests may not need justification, all requests have a better chance of soliciting a positive response if accompanied by convincing reasons. Likewise, denials of requests are more easily accepted if accompanied by reasons. In this task learners see and practice the language of such requests.

WHAT THE TEACHER HAS TO DO

1. Prepare a key of possible answers for Activities 1 and 2.
2. Adapt Activity 3 of the worksheet to meet your needs. If the worksheet is for use in a self-access center, you will need to refer to the center instead of the class. Wherever you use the task, you will need to react to learners' requests for changes.

LEARNER PREPARATION

Expose learners to additional formulaic speech for making requests and giving reasons.

VARIATIONS

1. For a speaking task, get learners to record their "reasons" on an audiotape. In Activity 3, record requests and teacher responses.
2. For pairs, ask learners to take turns asking and answering each other in Activities 1 and 2. In Activity 3, have them collaborate.

CONTRIBUTORS: Eric Bray teaches English at Doshisha University and Doshisha Women's College in Japan. Kenny Harsch is Director of English Education at Kobe YMCA College and teaches English composition and conversation at Kobe City University of Foreign Studies in Japan.

WORKSHEET

BEFORE YOU BEGIN

A request may or may not need to be accompanied by reasons, depending on both the request and the particular situation. For example:

1. I'm at home and feeling a bit cold. In most cases I can ask a relative without needing to state my reasons, "Could you close the window, please?"
2. I'm on a train, and the person sitting in front of the window is a stranger. I may need to add a reason for my request: "I'm sorry to bother you, but would you mind closing the window? The wind is blowing my newspaper."

ACTIVITY 1

Here are some requests. For each, think of two situations and write reasons to go along with the request.

1. "Would it be all right if I borrowed $199?"

2. "Would you mind if I went home early today?"

3. "Could I use your pen for a moment?"

4. "Could you answer the phone for me?"

ACTIVITY 2

Write a request and reasons for each of the following:

1. You're 10 years old and want to stay up until midnight to watch a movie on TV.

2. You're the owner of a small business and would like your employees to work overtime every day next week.

3. You work for an office and would like the management to buy word-processing equipment for your work.

4. You live in an apartment, and the person next door plays his stereo loud at night. You want him to play it softer.

5. You're a college student and want to borrow your parents' car for a date.

ACTIVITY 3

Think about our class. Is there anything you want me to change or add? Are there any books, magazines, and so on you want me to get for use in class? Are there any activities you don't want me to do anymore?

Write a request regarding our class. Be sure to include your reasons. (If your reasons convince me, I promise to grant your request.)

Writing Instructions

☑ beginner
☑ low intermediate
☑ intermediate
☑ advanced

☑ individual
☐ pair
☐ group
☐ tutor-assisted

☐ in class
☐ out of class
☑ self-access center

Aims: Learn the appropriate language and format for writing a set of instructions

Task Time: 20 minutes or more

Preparation Time: Variable depending on the availability of pictures and text

Resources: Computers for student use, total-deletion computer program, worksheet

PREAMBLE

This task shows learners the appropriate verb forms, sequencing adverbs, and format for writing instructions. It can act as a bridge between reading instructions and writing them.

WHAT THE TEACHER HAS TO DO

1. Add instructions for accessing the total-deletion computer program to the Preparation section of the worksheet. (In a total-deletion program—*Storyboard 2* is a popular one—a teacher-written text is presented to the learners, who restore the text by guessing the missing words.)
2. Add instructions for using the computer program to the Activity section of the worksheet.
3. Add a set of pictures of some kind of process (e.g., making a cup of tea, using a cash-dispensing machine) to the worksheet. Add any vocabulary items that you think learners will need to complete the task.
4. In the computer program, author a text that gives written instructions on how to perform the task represented in diagram or picture form on the worksheet.

LEARNER PREPARATION

Ask learners to give instructions for the process orally before they start working on the computer.

VARIATIONS

1. Give learners a jumbled set of diagrams depicting the process and ask them to order the diagrams before working on the computer.
2. Use the task to help learners write process descriptions.

REFERENCE

Jones, C. (1992). *Storyboard 2*. London: Wida Software.

CONTRIBUTOR: Sarah Carmichael is a Language Instructor in the Language Center of Hong Kong University of Science and Technology.

For this worksheet you will need to use a computer and the following program:

_____

PREPARATION

[Add instructions for accessing the program here.]

BEFORE YOU BEGIN

Look at the set of pictures below. Think about how you would tell somebody else how to carry out this task.

ACTIVITY

[Add instructions for using the program here.]

Use the pictures and the vocabulary to help you complete the written instructions on the computer.

[Add pictures and vocabulary here.]

SELF-ASSESSMENT

1. Do you feel satisfied with your own performance?
2. Did you have any problems when you were doing the task? If so, what are you going to do about those problems?

TASK EVALUATION

Do you think this task will help you write better instructions?

FURTHER SUGGESTIONS

1. If you had difficulty with the verb forms in the passage, look in a grammar reference book for the Imperative form or for reference material on sequencing adverbs, such as _first_ and _then_.
2. Try writing the instructions for something that you know how to do. For example, write instructions for how to use a piece of equipment or how to make something.

The Sequence of Events

Aims: Write coherently and with logical sequencing of events; read a literary text illuminated with visual references from video; explore the differences between a written text and visual interpretations of it

Task Time: 40 minutes

Preparation Time: Variable depending on the availability of short novels or readers and corresponding videotapes

Resources: Short novel, videotaped film version of the novel, videotape player, worksheet

PREAMBLE

This task helps learners logically sequence their writing and provides both listening and reading practice. Rather than simply writing a plot summary after having watched the videotape (or read the story), learners fill in the gaps by connecting the segments of text and videotape.

WHAT THE TEACHER HAS TO DO

1. Choose any short novel (probably abridged) and its corresponding videotaped film version (e.g., *The Great Gatsby*, *The Collector*). Scenes from both the short novel and the film should be clear and easy to follow.
2. Choose five or six 5-minute excerpts from the videotape and note the appropriate counter numbers so learners can easily locate them.
3. Choose five corresponding excerpts from the short novel.
4. Randomly label the excerpts of text Excerpt A, Excerpt B, and so on.
5. Tailor the worksheet to the videotape and novel you are using.

VARIATIONS

1. Develop a larger collection of worksheets for the texts and videotapes available.
2. Explore the differences between written and spoken forms of language.
3. Draw the learners' attention to the differences between the written and visual versions of the story.

CONTRIBUTOR: Elsie Christopher is an Instructor in the Language Center of Hong Kong University of Science and Technology.

PREPARATION

You will need:

1. Excerpts A–E of the novel _____ (stored in _____).
2. Videotape No.: _____ Title: _____

Make sure the videotape is rewound to the beginning.

ACTIVITY

1. Read through all the excerpts from the novel.
2. Watch the following excerpts from the video. After watching each one, find the matching extract and add its letter to the table.

From counter number	To counter number	Extract letter
[add numbers]	[add numbers]	
[add numbers]	[add numbers]	
[add numbers]	[add numbers]	
[add numbers]	[add numbers]	
[add numbers]	[add numbers]	

3. Imagine what happened between the excerpts. Write short summaries (three to four sentences) of what you imagine.
4. Summarize the excerpts (three to four sentences each).
5. Put all the summaries together in the right order to provide a summary of the whole story.

HOW WELL DID YOU DO?

Compare your summary with the novel, the videotape, or both to see if the summary is accurate.

FURTHER SUGGESTIONS

1. Compare the written excerpts from the novel with the videotape excerpts. Try to spot the differences in the presentation of the story. In the videotape, look closely at things like facial expressions, body language, accent variations, music, and so on. In the novel, look for things like descriptions, written speech, narrative details, and so on.
2. Try the same exercise with another novel and video.

An Ecological Approach to Argumentative Writing

☐ beginner
☐ low intermediate
☑ intermediate
☐ advanced

☑ individual
☐ pair
☐ group
☐ tutor-assisted

☐ in class
☐ out of class
☑ self-access center

Aims: Receive input on content, organization, and language for writing tasks; become sensitized to the principles of good essay writing

Task Time: 40 minutes–1 hour

Preparation Time: 2 hours

Resources: Feedback sheets on content, organization, and language for learners to complete; same sheets filled out by teachers; worksheet

PREAMBLE

Input on writing is very often given in the form of model examples provided by a textbook or constructed by the teacher. Such examples tend to focus on what is right, but it might be more helpful for learners to focus also on what is wrong with a particular piece of writing. This task, which relies on learner input, gives this dual focus to the assessment of writing, thereby raising learners' awareness of how to evaluate writing and alerting them to possible weaknesses. After the learners have produced their own piece of writing, you can feed it back into the system together with a feedback sheet and use it as input for future learners to comment on. This "ecological" approach to writing is an ideal way to build up the writing materials in a self-access center.

WHAT THE TEACHER HAS TO DO

1. Select five student essays on the same argumentative topic. They should range in quality from poor to very good.
2. Mark them using a standardized format (see Sample Teacher Feedback Sheets).
3. Produce a teacher feedback sheet for each one (see Sample Teacher Feedback Sheets).
4. Select a variety of other student essays.
5. Make two copies of each one.
6. Keep one copy unmarked. Mark the other using the standardized format.
7. Store the marked copies with their respective feedback forms.
8. Separately, store the unmarked copies with unused feedback forms.

LEARNER PREPARATION

Hold a session on how the standardized marking format works.

VARIATION

Use this recyclable approach to self-access writing for writing tasks based around other common organizational patterns, such as problem-solution or evaluation.

CONTRIBUTOR: Lynne Flowerdew is a Senior Language Instructor in the Language Center of Hong Kong University of Science and Technology.

PREPARATION

You need
1. The five essays and teacher feedback sheets on the following topic: _____
2. An unmarked essay and an unused teacher feedback sheet

ACTIVITY

1. Look through the five marked student essays together with the teacher feedback sheets. They will show you what constitutes "good" and "not so good" student essay writing. The samples range from "poor" to "very good" depending on the content, organization, and language. An outline of the essay is given to help you see the organizational structure. You will also see that the teacher does not correct students' language; instead, correction symbols are used to help students identify their errors.

2. Look at the unmarked student essay and complete a feedback sheet with an outline of the essay and comments on the most common language errors.

3. Collect a copy of the marked student essay and teacher feedback sheet. Compare these with the feedback you wrote. Is your outline similar? Do you mention the same language points the teacher notes?

4. Write a 500-word argumentative essay on one of the following topics:

    [Add topics here that are relevant to your learners.]

    *   Remember to brainstorm ideas and make an outline first.
    *   Make sure your essay is word processed and double spaced for peer review.
    *   When you have finished drafting your essay, use the following checklist to help you review the content, organization, and language.

Writing Checklist	Yes/No
Are the main ideas well supported with good evidence?	
Is the organization clear and logical?	
Does your essay correspond with your original outline?	
Have you proofread your essay for careless spelling and grammar mistakes?	

5. Ask a friend to comment on the content, organization, and language by completing one of the feedback sheets. Or make an appointment with a teacher to review your work.

6. Finally, give a photocopy of your essay and the feedback sheet to the staff in the self-access center. They will be added to the bank of student assignments to help other students with the writing process.

Thank you for helping us expand our writing materials in the self-access center.

SAMPLE TEACHER FEEDBACK SHEETS
(Teacher's comments are in italics.)

Outline	Content and organization
Introduction: attention-getter	*use of statistics (no. of cars on road) to highlight problem*
Thesis	*clear (yes, private cars should be restricted)*
Argument 1 + Supporting evidence	Increase in pollution results of EPD (Environmental Protection Dept.) survey
Argument 2 + Supporting evidence	Roads in Hong Kong will become gridlocked in 4 years' time Transport Department report (mentioned in SCMP 21/9/94)
Counterargument Supporting details	Might affect Hong Kong's booming economy *None—You need to explain how restriction of cars could affect the economy*
Refutation	Hong Kong's economy does not depend on transport *Logic—what is the link between transport and the economy?*
Conclusion: Call for action Consequences	Transport department should bring in new laws: otherwise, people's health will deteriorate *Why will people's health deteriorate? Explain.*

Comments: *I like the two arguments supporting your thesis—they sound convincing as they are supported by good evidence. Counterargument, refutation, and conclusion are rather weak—you need to provide a more logical explanation for the points you make. Conclusion could be strengthened by linking it to the two arguments.*

(continued)

Language correction code	Meaning
Prep	Wrong preposition
Punc	Wrong punctuation
Sen	Wrong sentence structure (comma splice, no main verb)
Sp	Wrong spelling
T	Wrong tense
V	Wrong verb form
WF	Wrong form
WO	Wrong word order
WW	Wrong word
^	Something is missing.
?	I don't understand this.
_ _ _ _ _	Express this more clearly.

Comments: *Although I understand what you are saying, there are some basic errors. Take care with sentence structure—there are a lot of comma splices in this piece of work. There is also misuse of some connectors ("besides," "on the contrary"). Avoid overused expressions, e.g., "on the other side of the coin," "hot topic," "it is undeniable that." Remember to proofread your work—some careless spelling mistakes!*

Overall grade: *C+ (average)*

Using More Descriptive Words

Aims: Learn descriptive words; practice using a thesaurus

Task Time: 20–40 minutes

Preparation Time: None

Resources: Thesaurus, worksheet, answer key (optional)

PREAMBLE

General words (e.g., *nice, say, good, interesting*) can be used in a variety of contexts. As a result, it is easy to overuse them, which tends to dilute their potency, particularly in writing. This task shows learners that using more descriptive words can make writing, and conversation, fresh and alive.

WHAT THE TEACHER HAS TO DO

1. Adapt the worksheet to suit your learners. Make examples and vocabulary items relevant.
2. After the learners carry out the task, look over the completed worksheets and comment on the learners' choices of more descriptive words, or prepare an answer key that shows a range of alternatives.

LEARNER PREPARATION

Familiarize the learners with a thesaurus in advance of this task.

VARIATION

Have the learners review their own writing and replace dull words with more descriptive ones.

CONTRIBUTOR: Kenny Harsch is Director of English Education at Kobe YMCA College and Instructor of English composition and conversation at Kobe City University of Foreign Studies in Japan.

WORKSHEET

Some words are general (e.g., *nice, say, good, interesting*). These general words can be used in a variety of situations, but they tend to lack power and exactness and can be boring, particularly in writing. For example, to say "That was a good movie" may be fine in conversation, but it would be poor writing for a movie review.

ACTIVITY

Underlined in the sentences below are words that are more descriptive than *good*. Complete the sentences with the names of movies you think fit the descriptions.

1. _____ is a <u>light</u> and <u>entertaining</u> movie.
2. _____ is an <u>inspiring</u> movie.
3. _____ is a <u>thought-provoking</u> movie.
4. _____ is a <u>masterpiece of cinematography</u>.

USE A THESAURUS

A thesaurus is a book of words with similar and opposite meanings. Writers use it to help find the right word.

For each of the sentences below, the underlined word is general. In the sample sentence, a more descriptive word is used. In *your sentence* think of another descriptive word. Use a thesaurus to help you.

1. It was <u>nice</u> of her to give you so much money.

    Sample: It was <u>typical</u> of her to give you so much money.

    Your sentence: It was _____ of her to give you so much money.

2. My parents' car is <u>nice</u>.

    Sample: My parents' car is <u>luxurious</u>.

    Your sentence: My parents' car is _____.

3. "I'm starving," he <u>said</u> to his wife.

    Sample: "I'm starving," he <u>whispered</u> to his wife.

    Your sentence: "I'm starving," he _____ to his wife.

4. She <u>went</u> home after talking privately with her teacher.

    Sample: She <u>trudged</u> home after talking privately with her teacher.

    Your sentence: She _____ home after talking privately with her teacher.

Look again at the sample sentences and your own sentences. Think of a situation that would fit each one. Are the situations different when the word is different?

FURTHER SUGGESTIONS

1. Working with a partner: Give each other a word in a sentence and then try to find a more descriptive word in the thesaurus. Be your own judges about which words are best. If you are not sure, use a dictionary to check the meaning.

2. Working on your own: In the future, when you are writing, take a little time to look for any dull or too-general words and replace them with better ones. More descriptive words can add life to conversation, too.

"In Brief" Revisions

Aims: Examine one's own writing critically to develop and expand on its content

Task Time: 25 minutes–1 hour

Preparation Time: Variable

Resources: "In Brief" section of a newspaper, worksheet

PREAMBLE

This task can provide learners with a technique or starting point for developing and expanding their own ideas when revising their writing. The technique is based on the belief that learning and understanding require critical thinking and that self- and peer questioning can facilitate such thinking.

WHAT THE TEACHER HAS TO DO

1. Collect "In Brief" articles from the newspaper. The "In Brief" section of a newspaper includes short articles (usually three to four sentences in length) about current news stories. If your resources include newspapers, have learners find their own articles. However, it is worth collecting a few articles yourself and writing keys of possible questions to expand the content of each. These samples can be used by lower level learners or as examples for any learner.
2. Adapt the worksheet to suit the needs of your learners.

LEARNER PREPARATION

For lower level learners, review *wh-/h-* question words (e.g., *what, where, when, why, how*).

VARIATIONS

1. Have learners continue to revise (three or four times) the "In Brief" article into a full-blown article or story.
2. In pairs, have one learner write questions, answers, or both for the other learner's "In Brief" article.
3. In pairs, have learners write questions and answers for the same article and compare their questions and answers with each other.
4. For groups, have learners play the roles of an editor and news reporters.

CONTRIBUTOR: Maida Kennedy Xiao is a Lecturer in the English Language Study-Center of Hong Kong Polytechnic University.

WORKSHEET

PREPARATION

1. Locate the "In Brief" section in a newspaper. This section contains short articles (three to four sentences in length) about recent news stories.
2. Choose an "In Brief" article that interests you.

BEFORE YOU BEGIN

1. Make a list of all the question words beginning with *w* and *h* that you can recall.
2. What do you think the phrase *to develop your ideas* means?

3. When a teacher tells you that you need to expand or develop your ideas more, what do you usually do?

ACTIVITY

1. Imagine that you are the news reporter who wrote the "In Brief" article and that your editor has told you to develop the article into a longer news story.
2. Write at least five questions about the content of the article that will help you make the story longer.
3. Answer the questions on a separate piece of paper and use the information in your answers to expand the article.

SELF-ASSESSMENT

1. Did you find any of your questions or answers more or less useful than others when expanding the article? If so, why?
2. Are you satisfied with the revision? Why, or why not?
3. Do you want to keep on revising and expanding your article?

TASK EVALUATION

1. How do you think you can use this technique in your own writing?
2. Do you want to do another "In Brief" revision exercise?

FURTHER SUGGESTION

Using this technique, revise a piece of your own writing for development.

Identifying Your Strengths and Weaknesses

- [ ] beginner
- [ ] low intermediate
- [x] intermediate
- [x] advanced

- [x] individual
- [ ] pair
- [ ] group
- [ ] tutor-assisted

- [ ] in class
- [x] out of class
- [ ] self-access center

Aims: Learn a system for identifying typical errors

Task Time: 20 minutes

Preparation Time: 20 minutes

Resources: Authentic text, worksheet

PREAMBLE

This task helps learners identify their strengths and problems in writing by making learners self-critical about their writing. Learners try to understand (not memorize) a passage selected by the teacher and then write it out without looking at the original. The contrast or contrasts between the original and the copy show the learner the area(s) in which they need either to seek help from teachers or texts or to internalize personal rules to deal with repetitive errors.

WHAT THE TEACHER HAS TO DO

1. Select a passage of authentic text suitable to your learners' level and interests. The passage can be from a few sentences to a few paragraphs long.
2. Label the text according to the level and the specific problems it presents. For example, it may have many prepositions, use a particular tense, or present key vocabulary and structures for English for specific purposes. The label helps learners find grammar exercises, rules, and other references after completing the exercise.

CONTRIBUTOR: Ken Keobke is a Lecturer in the Division of Language Studies in the College of Higher Vocational Studies at the City University of Hong Kong.

WORKSHEET

PREPARATION

For this task you need the following text:

Title: _____

Catalogue No.: _____

ACTIVITY

This worksheet aims to help you identify your own writing errors. Once you are aware of your errors, it will be easier to avoid them when writing. The label on the text indicates the language areas it contains.

Do the following things with the text:

1. Read the text several times until you understand it clearly.
2. If necessary, use a dictionary to look up any new words.

3. Cover the text and write down the time on your worksheet.
4. Try writing the text from memory.
5. When you are finished, note the time.
6. Compare the original with the text you have written. What are the differences? Where did you have problems? Are there several examples of the same error?
7. Write the main differences down and try to think of why you are having each problem.
8. Try the exercise again either today or later. Note the time it takes you to complete the task to show whether you are becoming faster as well as more accurate.

SELF-ASSESSMENT

1. Did you find patterns in the errors you were making? Did certain errors occur many times?
2. Do you think that now you are more aware of the errors that you typically make? What can you do about your errors?

Cooperative Dictation

Aims: Enhance comprehension by dictating meaningful sentences rather than isolated words; use dictation as an interactive, cooperative task

Task Time: 30–50 minutes

Preparation Time: 10 minutes

Resources: Five-paragraph text, worksheet, answer key

PREAMBLE

This task integrates three different learning styles: visual, auditory, and kinesthetic, which makes dictations more interesting and meaningful for learners. It also encourages learners to memorize meaningful sentences both when dictating and when writing. Group members cannot shirk their tasks, and they all try to do their best.

WHAT THE TEACHER HAS TO DO

1. Select a text that can be easily divided into five paragraphs of similar length.
2. Cut the five paragraphs apart and arrange them in random order on a sheet of paper.
3. Either attach the text to the worksheet or give it a catalogue number so learners can find it.
4. Make an answer key.

CONTRIBUTOR: Carmen F. Santás is a teacher in the secondary school Antón Fraguas de Fontiñas and a teacher trainer in the Institute of Education of the University of Santiago de Compostela, Spain.

WORKSHEET

This task is designed to improve your comprehension of a whole text (rather than individual words in a text). It also gives you practice in working together in English.

PREPARATION

1. You can do this task only in a group. The suggested maximum group size is five people.
2. You need the text called _____.

WHAT YOU HAVE TO DO

1. Divide the group members into
   a. someone who dictates
   b. someone who writes
   c. helpers (everyone else)

For each paragraph change roles so that everyone has a turn at each role.

2. For the first paragraph:
    *   The person who dictates has 1 minute *to memorize* the paragraph.
    *   After memorizing the paragraph, that person dictates the paragraph to the writer (without looking at the text).
    *   The writer writes the paragraph.
    *   The helpers orally help the writer (but they must not write anything).
    *   The writer stops after 4 minutes even if the paragraph is not finished.
3. Change roles and repeat the procedure for each of the other paragraphs.
4. When you have tried all the paragraphs, work together (without looking at the text) to guess at anything you did not complete.
5. Decide the correct order for the paragraphs. Add numbers to show the order.
6. Check the answer key to see how well you did.

A Smooth Flow

Aims: Develop coherence in writing

Task Time: Up to 30 minutes

Preparation Time: 30 minutes

Resources: Word-processing software, personal computer, text, worksheet

PREAMBLE

This task works on the hypothesis-testing approach of learning. Learners develop the concept of coherence in writing by working out the features of coherence themselves. They start with the level of their choice and work at their own pace.

WHAT THE TEACHER HAS TO DO

1. Select a text that is at your target level. It must have a clear, logical development of ideas and at least three paragraphs.
2. Save the text in a computer file named in a way that indicates it is the answer key.
3. Copy the file to a new file. Name the file in a way that indicates it is the exercise file. In this file, shuffle the paragraphs into random order.
4. Adapt the worksheet for the text you have chosen.

LEARNER PREPARATION

Make sure learners know how to use the word-processing software before starting this task.

VARIATION

Build up a collection of texts to allow learners to practice more. If you assign different degrees of difficulty to texts, learners will be able to find those that fit their level of ability.

CONTRIBUTOR: Eunice Tang is a Lecturer in the English Department at the City University of Hong Kong.

WORKSHEET

PREPARATION

1. To do this task you must be familiar with the word-processing software called [Add the name of the word-processing software here.].
2. Start up the computer, start the word-processing software, and find the following file: [Add the name of the exercise file here.].

ACTIVITY

1. The file you have opened contains a number of paragraphs. They are not in the correct order. Reorganize them into the correct order.
2. When you are ready to check your answer, look at the file called [Add the name of the answer key file here.]. It contains the original text.

CHAPTER 4

Listening

Many of the tasks in this chapter use authentic situations to help learners improve their listening skills. Detecting implicit and explicit cues, listening for the organization of information, and listening for gist are some of the aspects of listening incorporated into the tasks. As well as general listening skills development, several tasks focus on listening for academic purposes, and two use songs for listening practice.

Listening for Implicit and Explicit Emphasis

☐ beginner
☐ low intermediate
☑ intermediate
☑ advanced

☑ individual
☑ pair
☑ group
☐ tutor-assisted

☑ in class
☐ out of class
☑ self-access center

Aims: Learn to detect both implicit and explicit cues for salient information in authentic listening passages

Task Time: 10–15 minutes or more

Preparation Time: 20 minutes or more

Resources: Audio- or videotape, audio- or videotape player, worksheet, answer key

PREAMBLE

Being able to identify and use implicit cues can help learners comprehend spoken discourse. Not surprisingly, most learners have difficulty understanding information that is not explicitly marked. This task has learners focus on the various ways that important information is indicated in a listening passage.

WHAT THE TEACHER HAS TO DO

1. Preview a short (3- to 5-minute) audio- or videotaped passage from radio, TV, a documentary, a film, recorded conversations, or another source.
2. Write a simple list of important points and information from the listening passage. The points and information should be clearly identifiable in the passage.
3. Note how these points are introduced. Important information can be introduced either explicitly: with (a) a word, either a marker or meaning of a word, (b) an introductory phrase, or (c) an introductory sentence; or implicitly: with (a) louder stress, (b) longer vowels than normal, (c) repetition, using the same word or a similar word form, or (d) a longer, one-and-one-half- to three-beat pause; or both explicitly and implicitly in any combination of the above.
4. Prepare a worksheet.
5. Prepare answer keys for each section of the worksheet.

VARIATION

List the cues and write out the information indicated by the cues.

CONTRIBUTOR: Jim Bame is a Senior Lecturer in the Intensive English Language Institute at Utah State University, Logan, Utah, in the United States.

WORKSHEET

For this worksheet you need Audiotape/Videotape No. _____.

BEFORE YOU BEGIN

1. You should review implicit and explicit cues.
2. You should know what key words are.
3. You can work in threes, in pairs, or individually.

ACTIVITY

1. Read the information segments below. You may use a dictionary to help you.

Information segments	Implicit or explicit?
In Moscow there was a rally in support of communists and ultra-nationalists.	Implicit/Explicit
It was the biggest since the confrontation between protesters and Yeltsin.	Implicit/Explicit
Protesters shouted, "Hang Yeltsin."	Implicit/Explicit
Signs were present which said, "Yankee Go Home."	Implicit/Explicit
President Clinton will visit Moscow in three days.	Implicit/Explicit

2. Underline what you think are the key words in the sentences.
3. How will the information you underlined be indicated in the listening passage: implicitly or explicitly? Underline your prediction to the right of the statements.
4. Listen to the passage and find out whether the information was generally implicitly or explicitly indicated. Circle the correct word to the right of the statements.
5. Compare your answers with the answer key.
6. What was the exact way that the information was indicated in the passage? Listen to the passage again and write down the following kinds of information for each segment:

Explicit cues

a. Were there introductory phrases or sentences? If there were, list them.
b. Was the information indicated only by its meaning (with no markers or introductory phrases)? Write the information indicated in this way.

Implicit Cues

c. Were any words louder than other words? List them.
d. Did any words have elongated vowels? List them.
e. Were any words repeated? List them.
f. Did any words have longer pauses after or before them in this segment? List the words.

7. Now compare your answers with the answer key.

FOLLOW-UP ACTIVITY

In your journal keep a record of the use of implicit and explicit emphasis cues in various genres (e.g., TV news, radio news, soap opera interaction, movies, lectures, authentic conversations).

Predict, Listen, Organize

Aims: Identify a passage's information and organization; disregard information not in the passage and other irrelevant discourse

Task Time: 25 minutes or more

Preparation Time: 25 minutes

Resources: Audio- or videotape, audio- or videotape player, worksheet, answer keys

PREAMBLE

Most learners can answer comprehension questions by listening for specific information indicated in the questions but often have difficulty organizing the same information into a framework that shows an understanding of the main ideas and their details. This capability is important in understanding longer stretches of spoken discourse and is crucial in developing note-taking skills. This task enables learners to use their listening skills and think critically about the message they are hearing rather than translating individual words and phrases.

WHAT THE TEACHER HAS TO DO

1. Preview a short audio- or videotaped passage (3–7 minutes for class work, 5–12 minutes for lab work) from radio, TV, a documentary, or a film.
2. Write a simple list of points or information from the passage, either using the same language or paraphrasing according to the level of the learners.
3. Prepare a worksheet jumbling the order from the list made in Step 2, adding a few items of false information in the list and in other exercises.
4. Prepare answer keys for each section of the worksheet.

VARIATION

Use functions of language for various genres (e.g., radio commercials, TV news, lectures, social interaction) instead of the information itself. For example, for a lecture write the following on the worksheet without any other informational cues: *topic announcement, example, expansion—date, expansion—time, expansion—definition, expansion—unique information,* and so on.

CONTRIBUTOR: Jim Bame is a Senior Lecturer in the Intensive English Language Institute at Utah State University, Logan, Utah, in the United States.

Lectures

PREPARATION

For this worksheet you need Audiotape/Videotape No. _____.

1. Read the following list. You may use a dictionary.

Predicted order	Actual order	Topic
		coax cable
		three types of conductive media
		advantages/disadvantages of twisted wire
		fiber optics
		communications media
		advantages/disadvantages of coax cable
		security—defined and discussed
		twisted wire
		advantages/disadvantages of fiber optics

2. Predict the order in which the information will occur by writing 1, 2, 3, and so on in Column 1.

3. Listen to the passage and write in the actual order of the information in Column 2. One or more items on the list may not be in the passage.

4. Compare your answers with the answer key.

5. Listen to the passage again and write down what you find out about each of the following. One or more items on the list may not be in the passage.

Coax cable—

Three types of conductive media—

Advantages/disadvantages of twisted wire—

Fiber optics—

Communications media—

Advantages/disadvantages of coax cable—

Security—defined and discussed—

Twisted wire—

Advantages/disadvantages of fiber optics—

Compare your answers with the answer key.

Signpost Phrases in a Speech

☐ beginner
☐ low intermediate
☑ intermediate
☐ advanced

☑ individual
☑ pair
☐ group
☐ tutor-assisted

☐ in class
☐ out of class
☑ self-access center

Aims: Listen for signposting in a speech

Task Time: 30 minutes or more

Preparation Time: Variable according to the availability of a suitable recording

Resources: Video- or audiotaped short speech, videotape or audiotape recorder, worksheet, answer key

PREAMBLE

An awareness of the existence and functions of signpost phrases, such as *Now I'm going to talk about ...* and *Turning now to ...*, can help learners follow speeches, presentations, and lectures. Learners can also make use of these phrases in their own presentations.

WHAT THE TEACHER HAS TO DO

1. Find or record a video- or audiotape of a short speech (about 10 minutes).
2. Prepare a worksheet. Add the catalogue number for the tape to the learners' worksheet.
3. Prepare an answer key.

VARIATION

Provide a transcript of the speech with the signpost phrases blanked out. Have learners first read the transcript and try to predict what the phrase might be. Then have them listen and fill in the phrases.

CONTRIBUTOR: Sarah Carmichael is a Language Instructor in the Language Center of Hong Kong University of Science and Technology.

WORKSHEET

PREPARATION

For this worksheet you need Audiotape/Videotape No. _____.

BEFORE YOU BEGIN

Think about the following questions before you begin this task. What phrases can you use in a speech to

1. Introduce the subject?
2. Change to another topic?
3. Summarize and conclude?

ACTIVITY

1. Listen to the tape once without stopping it.

2. Rewind the tape to the beginning and listen again. Each time you hear a signpost phrase, complete a line of the table below.

Signpost phrase	Function of the signpost phrase
Today, I'm going to talk about ...	Introducing the subject

SELF-ASSESSMENT

1. Check your answers with the answer key.
2. If you missed any of the signpost phrases, listen again.

TASK EVALUATION

Was the task useful? Discuss this with a partner.

FURTHER SUGGESTIONS

1. Listen to more speeches, lectures, presentations, and talks and note down any examples of signpost phrases that you hear.
2. Prepare a short speech on a topic that interests you, using some of these signpost phrases. Practice the speech and then ask a friend to listen to you and comment on the effectiveness of your speech. Record your speech.

Names and Family Relationships

Aims: Learn Western people's names and different types of family relationships in Western countries

Task Time: 30 minutes

Preparation Time: Length of a TV serial drama in English

Resources: TV, video player, videotape of serial drama, worksheet

PREAMBLE

This task helps learners practice their listening skills in a focused way, become familiar with Western names, and begin to understand Western family relationships. Learners watch serial dramas on TV by themselves to become confident with the routine.

WHAT THE TEACHER HAS TO DO

1. In class, write and draw a typical Western family tree and include vocabulary relevant to family relationships (e.g., *married*, *single*, *divorced*).
2. Introduce the idea of serial dramas to the learners. Ask them what types of serial dramas they have in their own countries.
3. Write on the board the names of some Western serial dramas that are currently showing.
4. Give out the worksheet. Ask learners to watch several episodes of a serial drama of their choice and complete the worksheet by a given date. Add the date to the worksheet.
5. On the appointed date, arrange learners into groups depending on the serial drama they watched. Ask them to compare and discuss their answers.

VARIATION

Extend the task into discussions on different aspects of the serial dramas: theme, type of character, comparison with serial dramas in the learner's home country, and so on.

CONTRIBUTOR: Tom Farrell is an Assistant Professor in the English Department at Yonsei University, Seoul, Korea.

WORKSHEET

ACTIVITY

Choose a serial drama to watch. Watch three or four episodes of the drama and complete the information below.

1. Write down all the names of the people you hear speaking. Do not worry about correct spelling.

Speaker	Name
1	
2	
3	
4	
5	
[etc.]	

2. Try to decide the relationships among the people whose names you wrote in Step 1. Check the vocabulary your teacher gave you at the start of the session.

Speaker _____ is _____ of Speaker _____.

Speaker _____ is _____ of Speaker _____.

[etc.]

Prepare the information about the serial drama by [Add date here.] and bring this worksheet with you to class.

SELF-ASSESSMENT

1. Was this an easy or difficult task to do? Why?

2. If you had any problems with the names or relationships of the characters, how did you solve them? How did you work out the relationships among the characters?

3. Will you continue watching this serial drama? Why or why not?

Listening to a Song

☐ beginner
☑ low intermediate
☑ intermediate
☑ advanced

☑ individual
☑ pair
☑ group
☐ tutor-assisted

☑ in class
☑ out of class
☑ self-access center

Aims: Practice language and gain cultural awareness through music; evaluate a text

Task Time: 45 minutes

Preparation Time: 30 minutes

Resources: Audiotaped song, audiotape player, worksheet, answer key

PREAMBLE

This task helps learners appreciate the usefulness of listening to commercial music for language practice. The task not only enhances motivation but also encourages learners to transfer their listening skills to situations outside the language classroom. The task is suitable for all levels of learners, as children's songs and nursery rhymes could be used instead of popular songs.

WHAT THE TEACHER HAS TO DO

1. Audiotape a suitable song that includes sufficient information for learners to discuss or write about.
2. Write a tapescript for the song.
3. Prepare a worksheet and an answer key.

VARIATION

Compile a catalogue of song audiotapes and worksheets focusing on specific areas of language, for example, tenses, grammatical structures, and colloquialisms.

CONTRIBUTOR: Sue Fitzgerald is an Instructor in the English Language Study-Center of Hong Kong Polytechnic University.

WORKSHEET

PREPARATION

For this worksheet you need Audiotape No. _____.

ACTIVITY

If you are working alone, write your answers. If you are working with a partner or in a group, discuss your answers.

1. Listen to the song all the way through once before answering the following questions.
   - Is the singer one of the characters in the song?
   - How many other characters are there?
   - Are they male or female?
   - What is their relationship with each other?
   - How does the singer feel?

- How does the song make you feel?
- Does the song represent any particular culture?

2. Listen to the song again. Think about an occasion when you felt in a mood similar to that of the singer. Write a short account of the experience or tell your partner or groupmates.

3. Check your answers against the answer key.

SELF-ASSESSMENT

Was this task *easy*, *about right*, or *difficult*?

What your answer means:

- *Easy*: Try another song worksheet with a partner and discuss the answers to practice your speaking skills.

- *About right*: If you enjoy this type of task, try another worksheet.

- *Difficult*: Try another song worksheet. This time look at the answers first and see if you can then understand the song. Listen to the song as many times as you like.

FURTHER SUGGESTION

Listen to other popular songs and try to find some background information about the singers. Find out if the content of the song relates to some aspect of the singer's life. As a project, present the information to some friends.

Listen and Check
(Interview Skills)

☑ beginner
☑ low intermediate
☑ intermediate
☑ advanced
☑ individual
☐ pair
☐ group
☐ tutor-assisted
☑ in class
☐ out of class
☑ self-access center

Aims: Become aware of cultural differences in speech and English discourse patterns

Task Time: Variable

Preparation Time: Variable

Resources: Dialogue, audiotape, audiotape recorder, worksheet, answer key

PREAMBLE

This task makes learners aware of cultural differences in speech. Learners work with appropriate models accompanied by explanations of relevant parts.

WHAT THE TEACHER HAS TO DO

1. Select a dialogue to work on. Write the script for it and record it on an audiotape.
2. Look at the areas in the dialogue that your learners have particular problems with and write multiple-choice questions focusing on those areas.
3. Make an answer key.

VARIATIONS

1. To make the task easier, prepare a dialogue with gaps to fill in instead of asking general questions on the situation.
2. Work with a videotape instead of an audiotape. Focus on body language and what it means.

CONTRIBUTOR: Isabelle Gore is a Lecturer in the Language Institute at the City University of Hong Kong.

WORKSHEET

Job Interview

Select Audiotape No. _____ , Listen and Check.

Listen to the audiotape once without stopping. Then answer the following multiple-choice quiz.

1. When you go to a job interview, you should say
   a. Good morning/afternoon.
   b. Hello.
   c. Hi.
2. During the interview you should
   a. ask as many questions as you can.
   b. ask questions at the end.
   c. not ask questions.

3. You should
    a. ask about your salary.
    b. not ask about your salary.
    c. ask about the interviewer's salary.
4. You should answer questions
    a. briefly.
    b. lengthily.
    c. as you feel is right.
5. When you leave you should say
    a. Good day.
    b. Bye bye.
    c. Good-bye.

Stop and think before looking at the answer key. Look at your own answers. Can you explain why you feel they are correct?

Now look at the answer key and read the comments about each answer.

Directions From Memory

☑ beginner
☑ low intermediate
☑ intermediate
☐ advanced

☑ individual
☐ pair
☐ group
☐ tutor-assisted

☐ in class
☑ out of class
☐ self-access center

Aims: Review language for giving directions; follow directions authentically

Task Time: 15–20 minutes

Preparation Time: 2–3 hours

Resources: Audiotapes containing directions, audiotape players, blank map, worksheet, answer key

PREAMBLE

Giving directions is one of the hardest things to do, even in one's native language. In in-class activities learners usually direct each other around the room (or school) and complete an information gap activity in which one learner traces a route on a map while another gives directions. However, in authentic situations one person gives directions, and the other memorizes them or takes notes and then finds the place by following the recollections or notes. This task simulates the authentic situation.

WHAT THE TEACHER HAS TO DO

1. Make several answer keys from copies of the map on the worksheet.
2. On an audiotape, record directions from a point on the map called *X* to nine recognizable locations on the map.

LEARNER PREPARATION

In class, expose learners to formulas for asking and giving directions. Use this task as a follow-up to establish a close link between the classroom and the outside environment.

CONTRIBUTOR: Kenny Harsch is Director of English Education at Kobe YMCA College and teaches English composition and conversation at Kobe City University of Foreign Studies in Japan.

WORKSHEET

PREPARATION

For this task you will need Audiotape No. _____ , Directions From Memory.

ACTIVITY

On the audiotape are directions to nine different places. As you listen, write notes on how to get to each place below.

1. the post office
2. the hospital
3. the swimming pool
4. the bank
5. the department store
6. the supermarket
7. the library
8. the hobby shop
9. the bookstore

Look at the map. Your starting place is marked with an *X*. Use the notes to find each of the nine places on the map. Write the number of the place in the correct box.

[Add the map here.]

Look at the answer key. Were you correct? If you had any problems, listen to the audiotape again.

FURTHER SUGGESTION

Try to find a real-life situation today in which you ask a native English speaker for some directions.

Listen and Match

☑ beginner
☑ low intermediate
☑ intermediate
☑ advanced

☑ individual
☐ pair
☐ group
☐ tutor-assisted

☐ in class
☑ out of class
☑ self-access center

Aims: Become aware of differences in various aspects of speech; use a native speaker as a model for speech

Task Time: 20 minutes or more

Preparation Time: Variable depending on accessibility of native speakers of English with different accents

Resources: Audiotape, audiotape recorder, worksheet, answer key

PREAMBLE

Many learners find it relatively easy to listen to speech on a commercially produced audiotape. However, when faced with native speakers they have difficulty understanding, as they are not ready to listen to speakers with "strange" accents or to speakers who do not make allowances for nonnative speakers. This task helps learners practice their skills in listening to native speech in natural situations and with a variety of accents.

WHAT THE TEACHER HAS TO DO

1. Ask a number of native or near-native speakers to help you make an audiotape recording. Include a variety of accents and a mixture of males and females.
2. Record the speakers having a conversation.
3. Ask the speakers each to record some information about themselves.
4. Prepare an answer key for the audiotape.
5. Add the catalogue number for your audiotape at the top of the worksheet.

VARIATION

Compile a collection of similar audiotapes and worksheets on speech patterns to allow learners to spend time regularly trying to improve their listening comprehension.

CONTRIBUTOR: Lindsay Miller is an Assistant Professor in the English Department at the City University of Hong Kong.

WORKSHEET

PREPARATION

For this worksheet you need Audiotape No. _____.

ACTIVITY

1. Listen to the conversation on this audiotape and write down the number of speakers taking part in the conversation.

Number of speakers: _____

Number of male speakers: _____

Number of female speakers: _____

2.   Listen to the conversation again and try to decide the nationality of each speaker.

_____

_____

_____

Check your answers to Questions 1 and 2 with the answer key.

3.   Listen again to the audiotape (as many times as you like) and try to find some distinguishing features in the speech of each speaker. For example, Speaker 1 has many rising tones at the end of his sentences.

_____

_____

_____

Check the information about each speaker on the answer key. Were you able to identify any of these speech features?

4.   On the second section of the audiotape, the speakers who took part in the conversation talk about themselves. Decide which speaker's voice you like listening to the most and try to imitate that speaker's speech patterns. After practicing, make a recording on your personal audiotape giving similar personal information about yourself. Try to use the speech patterns you have been practicing.

RECORD YOUR PERFORMANCE IN YOUR SELF-ACCESS LEARNING DIARY.

Using Radio News

- [ ] beginner
- [x] low intermediate
- [x] intermediate
- [x] advanced

- [x] individual
- [x] pair
- [x] group
- [x] tutor-assisted

- [ ] in class
- [ ] out of class
- [x] self-access center

Aims: Listen to authentic spoken English; identify the topic; use predictive skills; reconstruct a text from notes and short-term memory

Task Time: 25 minutes–1 hour

Preparation Time: 20 minutes–1 hour

Resources: Audiotape, audiotape recorder, radio, worksheet, answer key

PREAMBLE

Many learners find two major problems when listening to authentic audiotape recordings: (a) they trip up on unfamiliar vocabulary and then find that they are unable to pick up the thread of the message again, and (b) they attempt to listen word by word, not a useful strategy with authentic recordings. This task is designed to encourage learners to use more appropriate listening strategies with authentic recorded speech.

WHAT THE TEACHER HAS TO DO

1. Record a news program off the radio.
2. Prepare a worksheet to accompany the recording.
3. Prepare an answer key to accompany the worksheet.

LEARNER PREPARATION

In class, introduce the learners to predictive listening exercises.

VARIATIONS

1. Make similar worksheets for other news programs from the radio or TV.
2. Have the learners do this task at home with their own radio or TV.
3. Set up a news corner in the self-access center with current newspapers, magazines, audiotapes, and other materials to facilitate this type of task.

CONTRIBUTOR: Bruce Morrison is a Lecturer in the English Language Study-Center of Hong Kong Polytechnic University.

WORKSHEET

PREPARATION

For this worksheet, you need Audiotape No. _____.
Low intermediate and intermediate students: Start at Stage 1.
High intermediate and advanced students: Start at Stage 2.

1. Make sure the audiotape is rewound to the beginning.
2. Set the counter to 000.
3. Read the entire worksheet and make sure you understand all the instructions. If you have a problem, check with another learner or teacher, or use a dictionary. Follow the instructions carefully.

BEFORE YOU BEGIN

Write down four topics, people, or places you expect to hear in today's international news program:

1.   3.

2.   4.

STAGE 1

Listen to all of the news program without stopping the audiotape.

- How many news stories were there?
- How many of the stories you predicted did you hear?

SELF-ASSESSMENT 1

1. Check your ideas with the answer key, with your partner(s), or with a teacher.
2. What do you think about the exercise (not the audiotape)?

What you think	What you should do
Very difficult	Listen to the audiotape one more time.
Difficult	Okay, do Stage 2.
Easy	The next time you do this task, go straight to Stage 2.

STAGE 2

Listen to the news again without stopping the audiotape.

- Check that you understand all the words in the box below. Use a dictionary if necessary.
- Listen to the news again, and for each news story (1, 2 ,3, etc.) put a tick under the appropriate story topic.

Story	Diplomacy	Crime	Military	Nature	Politics	Sports	Entertainment	Others
1								
2								
3								
4								
[etc.]								

SELF-ASSESSMENT 2

1. Check your ideas with the answer key, with your partner(s), or with a teacher.
2. Are you satisfied with your work on Stage 2?

What you think	What you should do
Yes	Okay, go on to Stage 3.
No	Decide if you want to repeat Stage 2, go on to Stage 3, or stop!

STAGE 3

Listen to News Stories 1, 2, 3, or all of them.
For each of these stories:

- Listen as many times as you want.

- Note down key words.

- When you have finished listening, use the key words to write a short summary of the story or stories.

SELF-ASSESSMENT 3

1. Check your ideas with the answer key, with your partner(s), or with a teacher.

2. Did you enjoy the tasks?

What you think	What you should do
No	Go and do something else!
Yes	Use this worksheet again another day with that day's news.

Student-Created Song Listening Library

Aims: Listen for enjoyment and practice in a pleasant atmosphere

Task Time: 5–30 minutes

Preparation Time: Variable

Resources: Booklet of song lyrics, audiotape, audiotape recorder, worksheet

PREAMBLE

This task helps learners practice their listening and guessing skills in an enjoyable activity. Songs are usually sung at about half the speed of normal speech, and most learners love listening to songs. When learners choose their own songs, they become more involved in the task.

WHAT THE TEACHER HAS TO DO

1. Make the worksheet and distribute it to the learners to get their contributions.
2. After learners contribute their lyric sheets, determine the cloze or masking procedure for each song. For example, white out every seventh word, the rhyming words, certain words you have targeted for their meaning or pronunciation, the first two or three letters of each line, the last letters of each line, or a line haphazardly down the middle of the page. Print the answers out on a separate sheet and then paste them to the bottom of the handout *upside down.*
3. Assemble the lyric sheets in a booklet.
4. Copy groups of 5–10 individual songs onto masters. (Note: In many countries, onetime copying for pedagogical reasons is allowed if no resale is involved. This exercise exposes learners to more artists, and when they like one, they usually buy the original. Thus the exercise, in a way, gives the record companies' artists more exposure. Nevertheless, teachers should check the copyright law where they teach.)

VARIATIONS

1. First use the songs in class and then put them into the self-access library, or put them directly into the self-access library.
2. Ask learners to record a short comment about the artist, music, or lyrics immediately after the song.

CONTRIBUTOR: Tim Murphey is an Associate Professor at Nanzan University, Nagoya, Japan.

WORKSHEET

Using Your Own Songs for Language Learning

In response to the question *How would you like to study English?* most learners say that they would like to use songs part of the time. I agree, and the best songs to use are the ones you like. So I would like to ask your help in collecting materials. I would like each of you to contribute one of your favorite songs for use in class or in the self-access listening lab. Follow the steps below.

1. Select a song you want to contribute. Write your name and the title on the teacher's Song Sign-Up Sheet (posted at the front of the class). Make sure first that nobody has already signed up for your song.

2. Make a copy of the words of the song on a sheet of paper. Somewhere on the page, add your own comments about the artist, song, words, or all of these. You can add pictures and drawings if you like.

3. Make an audiotape copy of the song. Put the song at the beginning of the audiotape.

4. Turn in the audiotape and the lyric sheet on [date] with your name on both. The audiotape will be returned to you.

I will make small adjustments to your lyric sheets (and use them in class) and put the songs in the self-access listening lab. Then you can listen any time you wish to. I am sure you will enjoy doing this task and listening to all the songs chosen by your classmates.

Listen for Gist and Take Notes

☐ beginner
✔ low intermediate
✔ intermediate
✔ advanced

☐ individual
☐ pair
✔ group
☐ tutor-assisted

✔ in class
✔ out of class
✔ self-access center

Aims: Listen for gist; negotiate the meaning of a passage

Task Time: 30–50 minutes (depending on the length of the tapescript)

Preparation Time: 5 minutes

Resources: Audiotape, audiotape recorder (or videotape, video recorder), worksheet, answer key

PREAMBLE

This task encourages learners to listen for the general meaning of a passage. Whether they pick up isolated words or complete sentences, they are constantly making predictions and evaluating their hypothesis by comparing it with their partners'. Learners also enlarge their vocabulary and become aware that one does not need to understand every single word of a passage to understand its general idea.

WHAT THE TEACHER HAS TO DO

1. Select a listening passage appropriate to your learners' level.
2. Adapt the worksheet to suit your learners.
3. Make an answer key.
4. If you are using the task in class, you might need to form the class into groups. If you are using it in a self-access center, you might want to remove Step 3 from the worksheet.

VARIATIONS

1. Use the worksheet with other kinds of listening passages. It helps learners enlarge their vocabulary and to process the different language items picked by different classmates.
2. In class, divide the class into four big groups. Have one group write down only verbs, another one nouns, the third one adjectives, and the fourth one whatever they can. Redivide the class into groups of four so that each new group contains one person from each of the original groups. Then have the class proceed to Step 2 in the worksheet.
3. To bridge the in-class and out-of-class activities, have the learners listen to the evening news at home and complete Step 1. Ask them to bring the worksheet to class the next day and hold the group discussion in Step 2.
4. Hold a whole-class discussion instead of the group discussion in Steps 2 and 4 on the worksheet.

CONTRIBUTOR: Carmen F. Santás is a teacher in the secondary school Antón Fraguas de Fontiñas and a teacher trainer in the Institute of Education of the University of Santiago de Compostela, Spain.

1. Complete the Step 1 boxes on your own.
2. Form a group with some classmates. Compare notes with other people in the group. Together complete the Step 2 boxes.
3. Form new groups, each containing one member from each of the old groups.
4. Compare notes again. Together complete the Step 3 boxes.
5. Check your answers against the answer key.

Step 1 → → → → → → → → Listen and take notes. My notes:	**Step 1** My predictions: I think this passage is about …
Step 2 → → → → → → → → Get into groups and complete this column. My group's notes:	**Step 2** First group's predictions: We …
Step 3 → → → → → → → → Form new groups and complete this column. New group's notes:	**Step 3** Second group's predictions: We …

When you have finished, discuss in your group the similarities and differences in the notes you made.

Follow the Directions

Aims: Listen to get information; use the information to perform a task

Task Time: 30 minutes

Preparation Time: 45 minutes

Resources: Audiotape, portable audiotape player with earphones or small audiotape recorder, worksheet

PREAMBLE

A language learning experience is most effective when the task is relevant to the learner, is easily transferable, and has the potential for use outside the classroom. This task combines all three elements: Learners go to a familiar district, follow audiotaped instructions, and answer questions.

WHAT THE TEACHER HAS TO DO

1. Prepare a worksheet that includes (a) a brief explanation and examples of directional vocabulary learners will hear on the audiotape, (b) an answer key for the exercise, and (c) the geographical starting point for the task (see Before You Begin on the sample worksheet).
2. Go to a familiar downtown district and record on an audiotape several step-by-step sets of instructions that direct the learner to go to designated areas and perform certain tasks.
3. After giving each set of directions, instruct the learner to listen to a question, stop the audiotape, and write a response. After the instructions, record several questions about the directions the learner has followed. The following is a sample transcript of recorded directions.

Activity 1: Start in front of the bookstore on the corner of King Street and James Street and listen to the first question.

    Question 1: Where is the bookstore located?

Activity 2: From the bookstore walk up King Street to Baker Street and turn to the left. You will see a bank next to the shoe store. Go inside the shoe store and answer Questions 2 and 3.

    Question 2: Find a pair of shoes you like. How much do they cost?

    Question 3: What is the cheapest pair of ladies' shoes you can find?

VARIATION

Using a map of a local area that is well known to the learners, record a set of instructions that direct the learners to mark certain areas on the map.

CONTRIBUTOR: David Timson is Associate Professor in the Faculty of Sociology at Kagoshima Keizai University, Kagoshima, Japan.

PREPARATION

For this task you need Audiotape No. _____.

BEFORE YOU BEGIN

Take this worksheet, the audiotape, and your portable recorder and earphones to the corner of King Street and James Street and begin the exercise.

ACTIVITY

1. Listen to the set of directions on this audiotape instructing you to go to a designated area in the city.
2. Write down the time you start the activity.
3. Follow the directions carefully and perform any tasks that are given to you. Listen to the directions and write down your answers.
4. Write down the directional words (e.g., *turn right, go straight, next to the ...*) you hear.
5. You have 30 minutes from the starting point to complete all the questions and reach the final destination.
6. Write down the time you finish the activity.

SELF-ASSESSMENT

1. Check your answers with the answer key.
2. Did you arrive at the final destination as instructed?
3. Did you arrive at the final destination within the 30-minute time limit?
4. Did you answer all the questions and perform all the tasks required of you?
5. Did you get lost? If so, go back and listen to the audiotape again.
6. After completing this exercise, do you feel confident that you can follow directions in English?

Listen to the Lecture

Aims: Practice academic listening skills

Task Time: 20 minutes or more

Preparation Time: 30–40 minutes

Resources: Text, audiotape, audiotape recorder, worksheet

PREAMBLE

One of the skills L2 learners at college most wish to perfect is the comprehension of academic lectures. For instruction in listening comprehension to be effective, and for learners to recall or retain the information presented, teachers, especially lecturers, must anticipate their L2 learners' receptive capabilities and provide adequately simplified input. The listening cloze dictation in this task helps learners not only practice their academic listening skills but also view lecture comprehension as a collection of integrative listening tasks that incorporate the characteristics of real-life listening situations and strategies.

WHAT THE TEACHER HAS TO DO

1. Select a section of text that includes a suitable topic for presentation, or prepare an original draft. Record the lecture on an audiotape.
2. Prepare a typed outline of the text or draft for the lecture presentation.
3. Prepare a learner worksheet that includes
   a. a cloze version of the lecture outline
   b. an answer key (a filled-in version of the lecture outline)
   c. a short vocabulary list (with definitions) of new terms or difficult words
   d. a list of comprehension questions concerning the content of the lecture
   e. an answer key for the questions.

VARIATIONS

1. Use the worksheet as part of a series of lectures on culture, literature, or other studies related to content-based instruction.
2. Use videotaped lecture presentations to acquaint learners with the discourse features and nonverbal communicative strategies relevant to academic listening.

CONTRIBUTOR: Stephen Timson is a Visiting Lecturer on the Faculty of Business and Commerce at Keio University, Tokyo, Japan.

WORKSHEET

The purpose of this worksheet is to help you practice listening to lectures.

PREPARATION

For this worksheet you need Audiotape No. _____.

BEFORE YOU BEGIN

Some of the vocabulary you hear may be new to you. Review the vocabulary list and refer to it during the lecture.

Vocabulary List
[Add vocabulary list here, e.g.:]

Senate: A lawmaking assembly. The upper branch of the U.S. Congress or most of the State legislatures.

[etc.]

ACTIVITY 1

1. Listen to the lecture on the audiotape and write the words you hear in the blank spaces of the outline (you can listen to the lecture more than once).

[Add cloze version of the lecture outline here, e.g.:]

Lecture Title: The United States Federal Government

I.   The Legislative Branch

The _____

Each <u>state</u> ... <u>two</u> ... <u>to</u> the <u>Senate</u>.

They are <u>elected</u> by the <u>people</u> for <u>six</u>-year ...

2. Now check your answers on Answer Key 1.

ACTIVITY 2

Try to answer the following questions based on the lecture.

[Add comprehension questions here, e.g.:]

How is the number of Representatives a state may send to the House of Representatives decided?

SELF-ASSESSMENT

1. Compare your answers to the comprehension questions with those on Answer Key 2.
2. If you missed anything, listen to the audiotape again.
3. Did you find these tasks easy or difficult? If you had any problems, consider doing a similar listening task once a week; you will soon improve.

CHAPTER 5

Speaking

Developing oral skills independently, without a tutor present, is an area most learners find difficult. The tasks in this chapter allow the learners to think about and plan their oral communication. The micro and macro speaking skills incorporated into the tasks include imitating intonation, speech rates, and pronunciation patterns; practicing the functional use of language; starting a conversation; and relating language to uses outside the classroom. Suggestions for monitoring and correcting speech are also included. In most of the tasks the learners work with partners to practice oral communication.

Suggestions for Effective Oral Presentations

- [ ] beginner
- [ ] low intermediate
- [x] intermediate
- [x] advanced

- [ ] individual
- [ ] pair
- [x] group
- [ ] tutor-assisted

- [x] in class
- [ ] out of class
- [x] self-access center

Aims: Cooperatively classify suggestions for oral presentations into five categories

Task Time: One to three class periods

Preparation Time: 20–30 minutes

Resources: Worksheet, answer key

PREAMBLE

Teachers usually introduce learners to the skill of presenting orally by suggesting the "best" way to prepare an oral presentation. Learners listen to or read these suggestions and promptly forget them because the learners have no involvement with the suggestions' content. In this short task the learners discuss and classify a list of suggestions into the following five categories: (a) how to select a topic and analyze the audience, (b) how to get information, (c) how to organize the information into a presentation, (d) how to practice the information, and (e) how to deliver the information to an audience.

WHAT THE TEACHER HAS TO DO

1. Make a list of suggestions about oral presentations (a useful text is Cummings, 1992), and use them to prepare a suitable worksheet and answer key.
2. Divide the class into small groups (three to six learners each).
3. Give out the worksheet and make sure that the groups understand that they must (a) define each category, (b) put each suggestion into at least one section, and (c) give reasons for putting a suggestion into more than one category.

VARIATION

Have learners do the first classification at home individually as a homework assignment. In class, form the learners into groups to compare answers and prepare consensus lists.

REFERENCE

Cummings, M. G. (1992). *Listen, speak, present.* Boston: Heinle & Heinle.

CONTRIBUTOR: Jim Bame is a Senior Lecturer in the Intensive English Language Institute at Utah State University, Logan, Utah, in the United States.

WORKSHEET

Classifying Suggestions

BEFORE YOU BEGIN

1. List the problems you have with giving oral presentations.
2. How do you overcome the problems?

ACTIVITY

1. On a sheet of paper make five sections called *Topic Selection and Audience Analysis*, *Research*, *Organization*, *Practice*, and *Presentation*.
2. Write a definition for each section.
3. Categorize the following list of suggestions for oral presentations by writing each in one of the five sections. If the suggestion applies to more than one section, write a reason for putting the suggestion into more than one section.
4. Use a dictionary if necessary.

SUGGESTIONS FOR ORAL PRESENTATIONS

(The list is not exhaustive.)

- Practice and time your presentation so that you do not go over your time limit.
- The audience determines how technical a presentation can be.
- Stand in a natural, easy posture.
- Avoid nonwords or words that fill pauses with no meaning, such as *uh*, *ok*, and *all right*.
- Exact wording is not important; there is no need to memorize all your presentation.
- Pause for 2 or 3 seconds after stating important ideas to emphasize them.
- Select a topic that interests you and fulfills the requirements of the presentation.
- Plan the use of visuals in your presentation.
- Do not use stories and anecdotes that would offend anyone. Avoid sexual, religious, and racial topics; instead recall a related incident from your past.
- Build the presentation around a few important ideas.
- Choose a topic that you already know something about.
- Know the information in your presentation thoroughly.
- Identify the goal of the presentation in the introduction.
- Use language that is personal, illustrative, and concrete.
- Develop statements that indicate what is coming next in your presentation (e.g., *the first thing I am going to talk about is X*).
- Interview experts or other people to get information.
- Write the words on visuals in black, dark blue, or dark green.
- Practice alone, in pairs, and in small groups. In other words, rehearse many times.
- Visit the library and find books, magazines, journals, and other materials about your topic.
- Feel and act confident; don't be nervous.
- Express your ideas in simple English; avoid jargon or technical language.
- Vary the pitch and loudness of your voice; in other words, avoid speaking in a monotone.
- Number visuals to make sure they are in the proper order.
- Make eye contact with individuals and small groups; don't look at the ceiling or the floor.
- Appear relaxed and fluid in your gestures and posture—not stiff or wooden.
- Take deep breaths before you deliver your presentation in order to relax.
- Use visuals for emphasis; do not use them as notes.

- Smile at your audience; they are not the enemy.
- Books may be useful to get information from.
- Use letters large enough to read on your visual and your note cards.
- Watch other people give their presentations; learn from their good points and their errors.
- Carefully prepare and practice your presentation, but do not write it out or memorize it.
- A question that you answer is a good way to begin the presentation.
- The basic purpose of an introduction is to gain rapport with the audience.
- Organize the content according to common and predictable organizational patterns based on the information and type of presentation; for example, *definition, example, chronology, cause-effect, comparison/contrast, process*.
- Imagine who your audience will be: age, sex, interests, education level, first language, and so on.
- Write a key-word outline on no more than three note cards.
- Relax; listeners cannot see and hear inside you.
- Have the main points firmly in mind.

SELF-ASSESSMENT

1. Did you agree completely with the other people in your group on the classification? Why, or why not?
2. Did you learn anything new from this task? If so, what?

TASK EVALUATION

1. Did this task help you think about the process of presenting information orally?
2. Were the suggestions helpful to you in your preparation for an oral presentation? Why, or why not?

FOLLOW-UP

Use the suggestions you have obtained by doing this task in your next oral presentation.

SAMPLE ANSWER KEY

Topic Selection and Audience Analysis
This means to decide who the audience is and what to talk about.
- Choose a topic that you already know something about.

Research
This means to find information about the topic.
- Books may be useful to get information from.

Organization
This means to put the information into the form in which you will present it.
- Use language that is personal, illustrative, and concrete.
- Write a key-word outline on no more than three note cards.
- Plan the use of visuals in your presentation
- Write the words on visuals in black, dark blue, or dark green. (Reason: so the audience can read them easily.)

Practice

- Pause for 2 or 3 seconds after stating important ideas to emphasize them. (Reason: so you can do so in the presentation.)
- Watch other people give their presentations; learn from their good points and their errors.
- Take deep breaths before you deliver your presentation in order to relax. (Reason: Practicing this will make it easier when you present.)

Presentation

- Relax; listeners cannot see and hear inside you.
- Pause for 2 or 3 seconds after stating important ideas to emphasize them. (Reason: so the audience easily understands the information.)
- Take deep breaths before you deliver your presentation in order to relax. (Reason: so you will not be so nervous.)

Speaking

WORKSHEET

The Five Senses

☑ beginner
☑ low intermediate
☑ intermediate
☑ advanced

☑ individual
☐ pair
☐ group
☑ tutor-assisted

☑ in class
☑ out of class
☐ self-access center

Aims: Learn to describe sensations, likes, and dislikes

Task Time: 2–3 minutes in class; variable outside class

Preparation Time: None

Resources: Learners' surroundings

PREAMBLE

This task allows learners to bring their outside world into the classroom, sensitizes them to their surroundings, and helps them learn how to describe their surroundings in a foreign language.

WHAT THE TEACHER HAS TO DO

1. Write *sight*, *sound*, *taste*, *touch*, and *smell* on the board. Ask the learners to talk about things they associate with each word and their feelings about each. An example is *smell: soup (good/delicious/plain/tasty)*.
2. Instruct learners to go to a public place where they will experience each of these sensations. Ask them to find a certain number of examples (e.g., two or three) for each sensation.
3. The next day, have the learners report back their experience (in pairs, in small groups, or to the whole class). Use the task to provide the class with precise terms to describe each sensation; rather than just *good* or *bad*, have the learners use terms like *gorgeous*, *sharp*, and *brilliant*.

LEARNER PREPARATION

1. Give each learner a sheet of paper divided into five parts, each with enough room to record one or two examples of each sensation.
2. Suggest suitable places to visit: for example, cafeteria, supermarket, outdoor market, restaurant, library, park, or garden.

VARIATION

Introduce some descriptive terms to use in the next class (e.g., "Find an example of something that tastes bitter.").

FOLLOW-UP TASK

Use this task as a basis for a written reaction (e.g., *the strongest sensation, what I like best about ...*).

CONTRIBUTOR: Dennis Bricault is Director of ESL Programs and Instructor in Spanish at North Park College, Chicago, Illinois, in the United States.

Preparing for Interviews

Aims: Practice oral interview-type questions in a social context

Task Time: 30 minutes (recording) + 60 minutes (worksheet)

Preparation Time: 15 minutes

Resources: Small, portable audiotape recorder, audiotape, worksheet

PREAMBLE

Most language learners want conversation practice, especially in preparation for interviews, but conversation with a native speaker can prove difficult to arrange or, when it does happen, can be stressful and one-sided. Learners often underestimate the value of interlanguage conversation practice because of a misplaced fear of "error swapping." In this task learners get to know each other and to appreciate the value of learner-learner interaction in the target language. The task stimulates transactional turns and interactive language in the context of interview-type questions. Learners practice asking and answering questions, clarifying, and confirming, and become sensitized to the concepts of turn and topic management as they relate to interviews.

WHAT THE TEACHER HAS TO DO

1. Arrange a sign-up list for the task, or get learners to arrange it themselves. Arrange pairs. (If learners repeat the exercise, they should choose a new partner.) Learners should not know each other very well.
2. Brief pairs on the value of this type of practice and the simple turn-and-topic analysis required at the end of the recording.
3. Go over selected parts of the interaction with the participants, focusing on turn-taking and turn-holding techniques as well as topic selection and handling.

CONTRIBUTOR: Mike Courtney is a Senior Language Instructor in the Language Center of Hong Kong University of Science and Technology.

WORKSHEET

PREPARATION

For this worksheet you need an audiotape recorder, an audiotape, and a partner.

BEFORE YOU BEGIN

1. Arrange to meet your partner in a quiet, comfortable place to make the recording. *Do not* prepare anything with your partner.
2. Insert a audiotape into the recorder and press *record*. Try out the microphone to get the best sound.
3. When you are ready, rewind the audiotape. Press *record* again and begin your conversation. Remember that you have 30 minutes for the interview and that you must not use notes or other prepared material.

4. Make sure that you both provide all the required information, or as much as you can before the audiotape stops after 30 minutes.

ACTIVITY 1

Find out as much as you can about your partner using the following topic headings. You can cover the topics in any order, but *do not* write anything down and do not plan what you will say.

1. Education	5. Favorite entertainment	8. Hopes for the future
2. Family life	6. Type of person you like	9. Experience of learning English
3. Hobbies	7. Dislikes	10. Working experience
4. Travel		

ACTIVITY 2

1. Arrange another meeting with your partner.

2. Listen to the recording with your partner. Discuss together how well you performed. In the self-assessment section below, circle the word that best describes your performance and give reasons. What do you both feel about your performance? Discuss ways in which you can improve your performance. Record the main points you need to improve.

3. Make another recording of an interview either with the same partner or with a different partner. Complete Step 2 again. Continue this process until you feel happy with your answers. If you have any major problems, ask your teacher for help.

SELF-ASSESSMENT

Interview 1	excellent	very good	OK	a bit weak	poor
Reason:					
Interview 2	excellent	very good	OK	a bit weak	poor
Reason:					
Interview 3	excellent	very good	OK	a bit weak	poor
Reason:					
Interview 4	excellent	very good	OK	a bit weak	poor
Reason:					

Building Thoughts

Aims: Speak creatively with picture prompts; work freely with a partner to improve speaking skills

Task Time: 1 hour

Preparation Time: Variable

Resources: Magazine advertisements, sheets of white paper, audiotape recorder, two blank audiotapes, worksheet

PREAMBLE

This task challenges learners to find ways to express their thoughts and feelings in the foreign language. It is done with a partner but in a nonthreatening environment, which lowers the learners' anxiety levels and frees their creativity.

WHAT THE TEACHER HAS TO DO

1. Prepare a set of thought-provoking prompt cards by cutting out pictures from magazine advertisements without the accompanying text and pasting them onto sheets of paper.
2. Place the prompt pictures in a file and clearly mark it *Prompt Pictures for Speaking.*
3. Prepare a worksheet.

VARIATION

Provide different levels of pictures for your learners but keep the tasks the same; the prompt pictures need not cover only complex themes.

CONTRIBUTOR: Robert Dwyer is an EFL tutor at Rajaphat Institute, Nakhon Ratchasima, Thailand.

WORKSHEET

PREPARATION

1. Work with a partner. Each of you select a picture from the Picture Prompt file in the Speaking section. Do not show your picture to your partner yet.
2. Select an audiotape recorder and place your personal audiotape into it.

ACTIVITY 1

1. Press the *play/record* button on the audiotape recorder and hand your partner your picture.
2. Partner: Begin speaking as soon as you are handed the image. You have 40 seconds to describe the image.
3. Keep track of the time and stop the recording when 40 seconds have passed. Please do *not* interrupt your partner and inform her or him of the time. Simply do your share of the task silently.

4. Once the task is completed, replace your partner's audiotape with your own, change roles, and repeat Steps 1–3.

ACTIVITY 2

Once you have both successfully completed Activity 1, work together to transcribe both audiotapes following the example below.

I can see a woman/ ahh / she's looking / ohh / she's under the sea / there's fish / star fish / ohh / she wear a beautiful earrings and then she looks like an executive / and there's another lady / wearing a red vest / and then / umm / she's very affectionate this lady / and she's wearing black pants / ...

Note: The slashes (/) represent pauses; the *ohh*s and *ahh*s are called *hesitations*.

ACTIVITY 3

1. Read your transcripts together.
2. Discuss with your partner how you can both improve your oral descriptions.
3. Look at and discuss each other's transcripts and listen to the audiotape while keeping the pictures for overall reference. Please do not write on your transcript or rewrite the transcript so that you can simply repeat it word for word back onto the audiotape. This would defeat the purpose of the exercise. Caution: Do not rewind your audiotape. Begin Activity 4 at the end of the first recording.

ACTIVITY 4

Once you and your partner feel confident that you are able to improve on the original recording, repeat Activities 1 and 2.

ACTIVITY 5

Call a meeting with an instructor. Give the instructor your individual audiotape and transcript of the two recordings marked *first* and *second*. Discuss your progress by receiving feedback on the two recording sessions.

FOLLOW-UP ACTIVITY

Write a descriptive essay based on the scene you have described. Use your instructor's feedback on the two recordings to support your writing.

WORKSHEET

Starting a Conversation

☐ beginner
☐ low intermediate
☑ intermediate
☐ advanced

☑ individual
☑ pair
☐ group
☑ tutor-assisted

☐ in class
☐ out of class
☑ self-access center

Aims: Practice conversation; develop awareness of appropriate conversational topics

Task Time: 25 minutes

Preparation Time: Variable

Resources: Audiotape of several native English speakers having short conversations, transcripts, worksheet, answer key

PREAMBLE

Learners often ask to practice "social English." This task enables them to understand which conversational topics are appropriate and which are taboo in Western culture. The follow-up gap-fill activity focuses the learners' attention on the structure of questions often asked in starting a conversation.

WHAT THE TEACHER HAS TO DO

1. Ask a number of native speakers to help you make some recordings.
2. Divide the speakers into pairs or groups of three. Give each speaker a role card including information about location, occupation, topic of conversation, and degree of politeness or impoliteness.
3. Explain that you want your learners to listen to conversations and decide whether the topics are polite or impolite. Ask the speakers to try to speak as naturally as possible. Supplying them with details of the context rather than a script should ensure a more authentic response.
4. Record four or five short conversations.
5. Prepare a tapescript. Blank out the parts of speech you want learners to practice.
6. Prepare an answer key.

VARIATION

Make a number of recordings of native speakers conversing about different topics. Activities deriving from these recordings could include cultural awareness activities, language practice, grammar practice, and role plays.

CONTRIBUTOR: Sue Fitzgerald is a Language Instructor at the English Language Study-Center of Hong Kong Polytechnic University.

WORKSHEET

PREPARATION

For this worksheet you need Audiotape No. _____.

BEFORE YOU BEGIN

Think about the following questions:

1. It is often difficult to start a conversation with a stranger, especially in a foreign language. Have you ever been in this situation? If so, how did you feel at the time? If you couldn't start a conversation or you found it difficult, why was this?

2. In Western culture people often start a conversation by talking about topics such as the weather. Do you know of any others? What are some of the topics used to start a conversation within your culture?

ACTIVITY 1

Listen to the conversations on the audiotape and note the answers to the following questions:

1. How did they start the conversation?
2. What is the topic of conversation?
3. Is it polite?

Check your answers on the answer key.

ACTIVITY 2

Listen to the conversations again and fill in the missing parts of the dialogues.

[Insert the gapped dialogue here.]

FOLLOW-UP ACTIVITY

1. With a partner, practice role playing the situations on the recordings. Try to continue the conversation for as long as possible.
2. If possible, videotape your performance. This will act as a record of your progress in addition to helping you with self-evaluation.

SELF-ASSESSMENT

Listen to or watch your performance with a partner or tutor. Discuss ways in which you could improve your performance.

Modeling Native English Speakers

Aims: Listen to and learn to match colloquial English intonation, speech rates, and pronunciation patterns; memorize modeled examples of English usage; increase English fluency

Task Time: 25–45 minutes

Preparation Time: Variable

Resources: Transcript worksheet, videotaped movie segment, videotape player and monitor, audiotape and recorder

PREAMBLE

All languages are dynamic. Although rules dictate language use, exceptions and accepted variations to these rules are countless. Books are good at giving learners the rules, but it is only through observation that learners will begin to see (and hear) the many ways English can be correctly used. Having learners listen to, imitate, and memorize native English speakers will help them remember the various correct uses of English and improve their English fluency and comprehensibility.

WHAT THE TEACHER HAS TO DO

1. Based on the desired degree of difficulty in intonation, vocabulary, rate of speech, and other features, select a 30-second to 1-minute segment of a monologue from any videotaped movie.
2. Transcribe the monologue (double spaced).
3. Indicate in the spaces between lines of the transcript where specific speech features are taking place. For example, above a statement made into a question by voice raising, place an upward-pointing arrow over the final few words; above an area where the speaker pauses, write *pause*.
4. Outside class or in the self-access center, have your learners listen to and observe the model videotape segment and memorize modeled speech features in an effort to sound like the model in all aspects.

LEARNER PREPARATION

Review macro elements of English speech phenomena, such as pause, lowering and raising of voice to differentiate key words and sentence meanings, speech rate differences, reductions, and contractions.

VARIATIONS

1. For more advanced learners, leave the macro speech markers off the transcript and allow learners to mark them themselves.
2. To check pronunciation and intonation accuracy, have learners record themselves and have teachers or classmates listen to the audiotape to see if they can understand it.

CONTRIBUTOR: Arron Grow is Director of the English as a Second Language Center of Mississippi State University, in the United States.

Introducing Topics Naturally

□ beginner
□ low intermediate
✔ intermediate
✔ advanced

□ individual
✔ pair
✔ group
✔ tutor-assisted

✔ in class
□ out of class
✔ self-access center

Aims: Learn how topics are nominated in natural conversation; explore these ways with various topics

Task Time: 20–60 minutes

Preparation Time: Variable

Resources: Conversation cards, worksheet

PREAMBLE

Introducing topics naturally in a conversation is a difficult ability to develop. It is largely a matter of developing a feel for what kind of opener works best to stimulate conversation and gauging the willingness of the other participants to respond. In this task learners read and practice common ways to introduce topics in conversation.

WHAT THE TEACHER HAS TO DO

1. Prepare a worksheet similar to the example.
2. Prepare a set of conversation cards that contain a title and a few pieces of information about topics popular with your learners. Or use conversation games from textbooks or teacher resource books (e.g., "The 'A+' Game," from Helgesen, Brown, & Mandeville, 1991, pp. 122–123; or "Tell Us About," from Klippel, 1984, pp. 82–83).

REFERENCES

Helgesen, M., Brown, S., & Mandeville, T. (1991). *New English firsthand plus: Expanding communicative language skills.* Hong Kong: Lingual House.

Klippel, F. (1984). *Keep talking: Communicative fluency activities for language teaching.* Cambridge: Cambridge University Press.

CONTRIBUTOR: Kenny Harsch is Director of English Education at Kobe YMCA College and teaches English conversation and composition at Kobe City University of Foreign Studies in Japan.

WORKSHEET

BEFORE YOU BEGIN

In most natural conversations, a topic is offered by one participant and either accepted or rejected by other participants. The diagram that follows shows the two options. Speaker A starts a conversation, and Speaker B either accepts the topic (left side) or rejects it (right side).

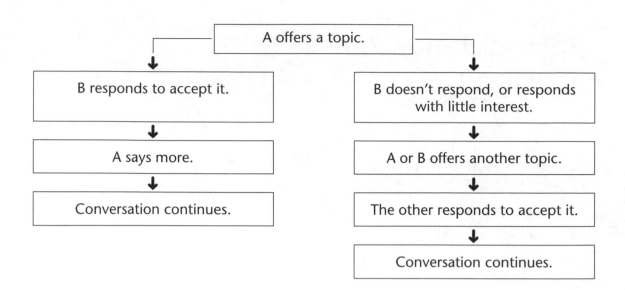

(Note: When you respond to someone's topic, it is very important to show that you are interested in sharing something. If I am silent when you offer a topic, or if my response does not show much interest, you might feel you made a bad choice of topic and abandon it. If that happens too often, you might give up trying to talk with me at all.)

Here are three common ways of introducing topics in natural conversation:

1. Real Questions and Statements

A real question is one for which I do not know the answer and that I am asking in order to find out. A real statement is one in which I think I am telling you something you do not already know.

A: How did you like *Schindler's List*?
B: Well, it was kind of depressing, don't you think?
A: Yeah, but that's a sign of how good it is.
B: Maybe so .... Using black-and-white was a good touch, wasn't it?

A: This book is great!
B: Yeah? What is it?
A: A book of short stories by William Saroyan. Know him?

2. Lead-in Questions

Lead-in questions are a gentle way of hinting at the topic. Almost all lead-in questions seem to beg for a short response (such as *uh huh*) as permission to continue introducing the topic:

A: (Do you) Remember that really tall guy we saw last?
B: Yeah. What about him?
A: I just found out he's my sister's new boyfriend!

A: Once I told you I used to be in a punk rock band, right?
B: Uh huh.
A: Well, today I brought in some of our songs. You want to see?

3. Rhetorical Questions or Statements

A rhetorical question or statement is an obvious (and sometimes ironic) introduction to a topic. It is different from a real question or statement; if I ask a rhetorical question, I'm not seeking an answer to something I don't know, and if I make a rhetorical statement, I'm not saying something I think you don't know; rather, I am seeking agreement or comment so that I can continue with the topic.

For example, one Tigers fan wants to talk about last night's game to another Tigers fan (the Tigers lost, 10–0):

A: Wasn't that a great game last night?
B: Oh, yeah. Really great. Kameyama was awful, wasn't he?
A: Yeah. It was like he had a hole in his bat ....

A: That sure was a bad game last night.
B: Wasn't it though? I couldn't believe it!
A: Me, neither. How can they play so badly?
B: I don't know ....

ACTIVITY 1: IN PAIRS OR SMALL GROUPS

Look at the conversation openings below. What kind of topic introducer is used? Write *R* if you think it is a real question or statement, *L* if you think it is a lead-in question or statement, and *Rh* if you think it is a rhetorical question or statement. Compare your answers with a partner's. If your answers are different, discuss situations in which either answer might be correct.

A: That was a fun test.
B: Oh, yeah. As fun as a funeral.
A: Do you think you passed?

A: Remember I was telling you about my vacation to Hawaii?
B: Yeah.
A: Well, I just got my pictures developed. You want to see them?

A: Have you finished the homework yet?
B: Yeah. Why?
A: I don't understand Question 3. Could you help me?

A: You know a lot about Japanese sumo, right?
B: A little.
A: What was the name of that guy who won over 50 straight bouts?

A: I just heard on the news that sales tax is going up.
B: Oh, no! Again?

ACTIVITY 2: IN PAIRS OR SMALL GROUPS

Get the conversation cards from the file. Pick a card and, as a pair or group, talk about the topic on the card. Explore different ways of introducing topics.

Understanding and Discussing Political Cartoons

Aims: Interpret political cartoons; practice speaking by discussing the cartoons

Task Time: Open ended

Preparation Time: Minimal

Resources: Speaking corner, pen, paper, worksheet, audiotape (optional), recorder (optional)

PREAMBLE

Political cartoons have a number of useful attributes for language learning. Their visual impact engages the learner's attention, their humor helps learners enjoy the task, they are topical, they contain rich visual (and sometimes verbal) imagery, and they are almost without exception trenchantly critical of people in power. The activities in this task rehearse both standard language patterns and more speculative, analytical, and discursive skills. Learners are encouraged to use their knowledge of the world and to express their opinions. Closed answers have deliberately been avoided.

WHAT THE TEACHER HAS TO DO

1. Adapt the worksheet.
2. Select a cartoon. Cut it out and paste it onto a sheet of paper. Attach the cartoon to the worksheet and put it in the self-access center.
3. Monitor the success of the material orally or via write-ups from the learners.

LEARNER PREPARATION

If necessary, demonstrate the task as a class exercise before providing it for self-directed learning.

CONTRIBUTOR: George Kershaw is a freelance EFL specialist in Manchester, United Kingdom.

WORKSHEET

BEFORE YOU BEGIN

Find a partner to work with. (You may want to record your discussion on an audiotape.)

ACTIVITY

Work with the newspaper cartoon attached. Describe the cartoon to your partner. Do not allow your partner to see the cartoon but ask him or her to draw what you describe.

Stage 1: Description (Picture Dictation)

Has this ever happened to you? You bump into a friend or colleague and want to tell her about a really good cartoon you saw in the newspaper. You describe it to her. This is what you are going to do now with your partner, but please do not try to interpret the cartoon at this stage. You are going to describe the cartoon so well and in such detail that your partner will be able to draw it. Here are some description cue questions that will help you describe it.

- What is in the foreground of the cartoon?
- What is in the background of the cartoon?
- What is at the center/on the left/right of/at the top/bottom of the cartoon?
- Is it day or night?
- What season is it? How do you know?
- How many people are in the cartoon?
- What do they look like (e.g., young/old, fat/thin, nationality, scruffy/smart, happy/sad)?
- Who are they meant to be? How do you know?
- What are they doing to each other?
- What are they saying to each other?
- Where is the cartoon taking place?
- How is the scene set? What details tell you where this is taking place?
- Apart from the people, what other things can you see in the cartoon?

Now describe the cartoon to your partner so that your partner can draw it. When your partner is ready, check the sketch against the original cartoon. Don't be too critical: If your partner got it wrong, it was probably your fault!

Stage 2: Analysis—What the Cartoon Means

You and your partner have a good idea of what the cartoon looks like by now, but what does it mean? With your partner, try to decide what the cartoonist is trying to say—the *message* of the cartoon. Below are some cue questions to guide your thinking.

- What current events is the cartoonist referring to?
- Why has the cartoonist chosen this particular setting?
- Why has the cartoonist chosen to portray these particular characters?
- A political cartoon is almost always critical. Who is the cartoonist trying to criticize?
- Whose side is the cartoonist on, in your opinion?
- Is the cartoon funny? If so, what makes it funny? If not, why not?
- Besides entertaining the reader, what is the cartoonist trying to do? to warn the reader? to expose someone important? to ridicule an action or an attitude?
- What do you think is the attitude of the cartoonist toward the issue depicted in the cartoon?
- Is the cartoon fair?

If you were the person(s) criticized in the cartoon and had the opportunity to draw a cartoon in reply, what would you draw? If you can, draw it!

Stage 3: Feedack

You would benefit at this stage from some feedback on your work from a teacher or self-access tutor. You have three options:

1. Ask the self-access tutor to listen to your verbal summary of the cartoon and its meaning.
2. Record your discussion and your summaries on an audiotape and give them to the self-access tutor or your class teacher.

Understanding and Discussing Political Cartoons

3. Write up your discussion and give the account to the self-access tutor or your class teacher for appraisal.

ONE FINAL WORD

If you like this kind of cartoon and find a good example in your newspaper reading, copy it and bring it in to your class teacher or self-access center tutor. We can use it to provide materials for other learners.

A Simulation to Practice Agreeing and Disagreeing

☐ beginner
☐ low intermediate
☑ intermediate
☑ advanced

☐ individual
☐ pair
☑ group
☐ tutor-assisted

☑ in class
☐ out of class
☑ self-access center

Aims: Practice agreeing and disagreeing

Task Time: 30 minutes

Preparation Time: 15 minutes

Resources: Role cards, handout, audiotape (optional), recorder (optional)

PREAMBLE

This task involves learner cooperation. Three learners work together to practice spoken communication: agreeing and disagreeing on controversial issues.

WHAT THE TEACHER HAS TO DO

1. Prepare a handout with instructions for the task.
2. Prepare a set of three role cards for the task and put them in an envelope attached to the handout.

VARIATIONS

1. Prepare as many sets of role cards as you wish to accompany the generic handout.
2. Ask your learners to think of situations they want to talk about and prepare some corresponding simulation cards.

CONTRIBUTOR: Wai-king Tsang is Assistant Professor in the English Department at the City University of Hong Kong.

WORKSHEET

SAMPLE HANDOUT

Instructions for learners

1. Work with two partners. You will all role play and discuss a controversial issue.
2. Open the envelope and have each partner study one role card. Do not show your card to your two partners.
3. Try to discuss the topic for at least 20 minutes. Try to end up with some sort of conclusion to the problem. If you wish, record your conversation on an audiotape.
4. If you made an audiotape, listen to it afterwards. Assess each other's language skills, look for strengths and weaknesses, and discuss how you could improve your discussion.

WORKSHEET

Role A

Together with your partners, choose a country or city to talk about. You are a spokesman representing the Tourist Association. You have been friends with B (a sociologist) since school days. Both of you have just finished dinner with C (an overseas friend) and started a conversation about tourism: Is tourism a good thing?

You think that the amount of money the association spends is worth the benefits your country gains from a healthy tourist industry, such as

- employment opportunities
- use of hotel facilities by local people
- ability to attract businessmen to invest in your country.

Role B

Together with your partners, choose a country or city to talk about. You are a sociologist. You have been friends with A (a spokesman representing the Tourist Association) since school days. Both of you have just finished dinner with C (an overseas friend) and started a conversation about tourism: Is tourism a good thing?

You feel that the tourist association spends too much on overseas promotion.

- The money could be better spent on social services.
- Imported lifestyles, moral values, and behavior may have a disruptive effect on the discipline of the young.

Role C

Together with your partners, choose a country or city to talk about. You are a tourist. You are an overseas friend of A (a spokesman representing the Tourist Association) and B (a sociologist). You have come on a visit for a week. You have just finished dinner with A and B and started a conversation about tourism: Is tourism a good thing?

You are able to give a firsthand impression of the country.

- You give your opinion on whether you like to visit the country.
- Your opinion can be favorable, unfavorable, or mixed.

A Call to Dr. Know-it-all

Aims: Practice eliciting opinions and suggestions, giving opinions, and making suggestions

Task Time: 20 minutes

Preparation Time: 15–20 minutes

Resources: Role cards, handout, audiotape (optional), recorder (optional)

PREAMBLE

In this task two learners work together to practice spoken communication by simulating a discussion between the host of a call-in radio show and a caller with a problem.

WHAT THE TEACHER HAS TO DO

1. Prepare a handout with instructions for the task.
2. Prepare role cards for the task. Place each in an envelope.

LEARNER PREPARATION

This role play works well after a class session on opinions and suggestions.

VARIATIONS

1. Have the learners prepare their own role cards and place them in a box for others to use.
2. Ask the learners to audiotape their conversation, listen to it, and assess how well they perform.

CONTRIBUTOR: Matilda Wong is a Lecturer in the English Department at the City University of Hong Kong.

WORKSHEET

SAMPLE HANDOUT

Instructions

1. Work with your partner. Sit back-to-back so that you cannot see each other.
2. You will be role playing a midnight phone-in radio program:

   Are you troubled? Are you worried?

   Make a call to Dr. Know-it-all.

   This is a midnight program, so talk quietly but be audible. You will have unequal roles. The Doctor will initiate the conversation, but you should have an equal amount of participation.
3. Open the envelope and study your role card. Do not show it to your partner.

4. Dr. Know-it-all should start the conversation.

5. Try to keep your conversation going for about 10 minutes.

SAMPLE ROLE CARDS

Role A

You are Dr. Know-it-all, the host of a midnight phone-in radio program. Listen to the incoming call and give opinions or make suggestions to the caller.

Role B

Call Dr. Know-it-all and ask for opinions and suggestions about the following problem:

- You had a good time with your ex-boyfriend or -girlfriend (classy restaurants, expensive shows).
- He or she is too serious about love.
- You never thought of marrying him or her.
- You finally got fed up as he or she would not leave you alone.

CHAPTER 6

Vocabulary

The tasks in this chapter enrich learners' general, professional, and academic vocabulary. Featured in many of the tasks are ways for learners to keep track of their vocabulary development with diaries and vocabulary tables and build up their stock of new words using pictures, sounds, thesauruses, and dictionaries. Other tasks encourage learners to think about how different English-speaking communities use vocabulary in different ways and to explore their own feelings and attitudes toward the use of words.

Draw and Describe

☑ beginner
☑ low intermediate
☑ intermediate
☐ advanced

☑ individual
☐ pair
☐ group
☐ tutor-assisted

☐ in class
☐ out of class
☑ self-access center

Aims: Practice vocabulary used in giving a physical description of a person

Task Time: 20 minutes

Preparation Time: 30 minutes

Resources: Simple pictures of people's faces, vocabulary list, prepared audiotape, audiotape recorder, worksheet

PREAMBLE

Learning to describe people can present difficulties because of the amount of vocabulary needed. Often, describing people is an in-class activity, but sometimes learners can feel uncomfortable describing each other. This task gives them extra practice out of class and does not involve describing their classmates.

WHAT THE TEACHER HAS TO DO

1. Draw or cut out from magazines pictures of people's faces.
2. Paste the pictures onto standardized cards.
3. On the back of each card write a detailed description of the person in the picture.
4. Make an audiotape of the description.
5. Prepare a worksheet to accompany the cards.
6. Prepare a target vocabulary list to accompany the cards.
7. Place the cards, vocabulary list, audiotape, and worksheet together in an envelope and mark it *Faces*.

VARIATIONS

1. Make up different packs of cards on other topics, such as transport, animals, and sports.
2. Ask learners to find pictures and write the descriptions as above to build up a picture library for descriptions.

CONTRIBUTOR: Eric Bray teaches English at Doshisha University and Doshisha Women's College in Japan.

WORKSHEET

PREPARATION

You need Audiotape No. _____, Faces.

BEFORE YOU BEGIN

Look at the vocabulary list with this pack of cards. If it includes words that you do not know, look them up in your dictionary before you begin.

Vocabulary

Hair: *straight, wavy, curly, long, shoulder length, short, thin, bald*
Hair color: *black, brown, light brown, blond, red, gray, salt and pepper*

Eyes: *big, small, narrow, almond-shaped*
Eye color: *black, brown, blue, green, hazel*

Eyebrows: *bushy, thin, straight, arched*

Nose: *turned-up, flat, prominent, broad*

ACTIVITY

Listen to the descriptions of the people on the audiotape and try to draw pictures of them.

SELF-ASSESSMENT

When you have finished your drawings, look at the pictures on the cards. How close are your drawings to the pictures?

Very close	Good. You have no real problems listening to descriptions of people. Try another set of description cards.
So-so	OK. Listen to the audiotape again and think of how you need to change your drawings so that they are the same as the pictures
Not very close at all	Go back to the vocabulary list and study it carefully. If you do not fully understand any of the words, get some help from your teacher. Then try the activity again.

Replace the
Nonsense Words

Aims: Think about the structure of language; guess the meaning of unknown words in context

Task Time: 20 minutes

Preparation Time: 10 minutes

Resources: Text, worksheet, answer key

PREAMBLE

All too often, learners fail to look for the meaning of unknown vocabulary because they lack the strategies to do so. By working with nonsense words in this task, learners can focus on the strategy of guessing meaning and grammatical structure from context rather than on the words themselves.

WHAT THE TEACHER HAS TO DO

1. Select a text suitable for the level of your learners. If you wish, choose a text that includes grammatical structures or vocabulary you want to focus on.
2. Blank out the relevant words and replace them with the 10 nonsense words from the worksheet.
3. Attach the text to the worksheet.
4. Prepare an answer key.

LEARNER PREPARATION

If you wish, preteach the vocabulary with a matching activity.

CONTRIBUTOR: Sue Fitzgerald is a Language Instructor in the English Language Study-Center of Hong Kong Polytechnic University.

ACTIVITY

Read the text that is attached to this worksheet. As you read it, complete as much of the following table as you can.

Word	Part of speech	Meaning	Synonym
jamba			
cassy			
pindu			
opit			
foogle			
halory			
wut			
deted			
koofy			

SELF-ASSESSMENT

1. Check your answers with the answer key.
2. Go through the text again and think about how the structure of the sentence helped you find the correct word.
3. Did looking at the word in context help you understand the meaning? What other reading strategies did you use? Make a list of these and add new strategies to the list as you discover yourself using them.

Contextualized Business Vocabulary

☐ beginner
☐ low intermediate
☑ intermediate
☐ advanced

☑ individual
☐ pair
☐ group
☐ tutor-assisted

☐ in class
☐ out of class
☑ self-access center

Aims: Examine contextualized examples of vocabulary items commonly used in report writing

Task Time: 30–40 minutes

Preparation Time: Variable

Resources: Computer, concordancing program, computerized corpus of business reports, tutorial sheet on concordancing, worksheet, answer key

PREAMBLE

This task shows how certain vocabulary items commonly used in report writing are used in context. Although learners undoubtedly know the meaning of such items as *survey* and *need*, they often are unsure which verbs or prepositions such items collocate with, resulting in usages like *make a survey* and *there is a need of* instead of *conduct/carry out a survey* and *there is a need for*. By using a concordancer to obtain a key-word-in-context frequency list of such items and the viewfinder option to examine the items in a wider context, learners become sensitized to this problematic area of collocation.

WHAT THE TEACHER HAS TO DO

1. Become familiar with concordancing techniques for computer-assisted language learning. A good starting point is the *Longman Mini-Concordancer Handbook*; two concordancing programs are *Longman Mini-Concordancer* and *MicroConcord*.
2. Compile a computerized corpus of recommendation reports. A corpus of about 15,000 words, consisting of approximately 20 short reports of about 750 words each, is ideal for concordancing purposes.
3. Prepare a tutorial sheet to teach learners the principles of concordancing.
4. Devise a worksheet for vocabulary items.
5. Prepare an answer key for the worksheet.

VARIATION

Devise similar worksheets on the collocation of nouns with certain adverbs in a business context based on the collection of business newspaper articles that forms a subcorpus of the *MicroConcord* corpus collection.

REFERENCES

Longman mini-concordancer [Computer software]. (1989). Harlow, England: Longman.
Longman mini-concordancer handbook [Computer software manual]. (1989). Harlow, England: Longman.
Scott, M., & Johns, T. (1993). *MicroConcord* [Computer software]. Oxford: Oxford University Press.

CONTRIBUTOR: Lynne Flowerdew is a Senior Language Instructor in the Language Center of Hong Kong University of Science and Technology.

Report Writing

PREPARATION

Make sure you know how to use the concordancing software.

ACTIVITY

Stage 1

Before using the software to look at the vocabulary items in context, write down which verbs or prepositions you think are used with the following nouns. There may be more than one correct choice for each noun.

Which verbs are used?	What I think	What the concordancer says
survey		
questionnaire		
findings		
approval		
measures		

Which prepositions are used?	What I think	What the concordancer says
need		
solution		
data		
factor		
benefits		

Stage 2

1. Look at the nouns in context using the *Longman Mini-Concordancer.*
2. Which verbs and prepositions are most commonly used with the above nouns? Write the most common expressions in the third column above.
3. How many of the verbs given by the concordancer are in the passive? What does this tell you about style in report writing?
4. Does the meaning of the nouns change if a different preposition is used with them (e.g., *benefits for, benefits of*)?

SELF-ASSESSMENT

Check the answer key. How many of the verbs and prepositions you chose are the same as the ones suggested by the concordancer?

FURTHER SUGGESTIONS

Use the computerized report-writing material to check how other items are used in context.

SAMPLE ANSWER KEY

Which verbs are used?	What the concordancer says
survey	I was asked to carry out a survey on
questionnaire	A questionnaire was administered to
findings	This report will present/discuss the findings
approval	I request that approval be given for
measures	If these measures are not implemented/taken, then

Which prepositions are used?	What the concordancer says
need	There is a need for more
solution	I will evaluate three alternative solutions for this problem
data	Data on _____ are shown below
factor	These are major factors in our decision.
benefits	The benefits for our company are enormous.

Vocabulary in Context

☐ beginner
☐ low intermediate
☑ intermediate
☑ advanced

☑ individual
☐ pair
☐ group
☐ tutor-assisted

☑ in class
☑ out of class
☑ self-access center

Aims: Enrich vocabulary

Task Time: 20 minutes or more

Preparation Time: 15 minutes

Resources: Newspaper or magazine article, worksheet, answer key

PREAMBLE

Using an authentic text for vocabulary enrichment helps learners develop a sense of the power of a rich vocabulary. This task encourages learners to investigate synonyms and to avoid false cognates, and is a quick way of developing vocabulary exercises. The learners' worksheets may provide extra information for future answer keys.

WHAT THE TEACHER HAS TO DO

1. Select a newspaper or magazine article that is at a suitable level of difficulty for your learners and contains vocabulary that will be useful to them.
2. Select the vocabulary items you want the learners to focus on.
3. Copy the items into the first column of the worksheet.
4. Photocopy the worksheet and label it *Answer Key*.
5. Add as many items as you can to the second column of the answer key. (A thesaurus would make this a quick job.)
6. Attach the article (and the answer key) to the worksheet. In some countries it is necessary to obtain permission to copy newspaper articles. For this task you can use the original article; it might be wise to laminate it for durability.

VARIATION

Use this exercise to practice either different classes of words or a random selection of items.

CONTRIBUTOR: David Gardner is a Senior Language Instructor in the English Center of the University of Hong Kong.

WORKSHEET

ACTIVITY

1. In the first column of the table below are a number of words that appear in the attached newspaper article. Look for them in the article and study the context in which they are used.
2. In the second column of the table, add as many words as you can that have a similar meaning. Only add words that are valid in the same context.

Word	Meaning
1. durable	*lasting, tough; opposite of temporary*
2.	
3.	
4.	
5.	
6.	
7.	
8.	
9.	
10.	
11.	
12.	
13.	
14.	
15.	
16.	
17.	
18.	
19.	
20.	

HOW WELL DID YOU DO?

1. When you have finished, check your answers with the answer key.
2. If the answer key has words that you do not know, use a dictionary to check their meaning.
3. If you have written down words that are not on the answer key, use a dictionary to see if the meaning is correct.

British English–American English: What's the Difference?

Aims: Explore the vocabulary of different Englishes

Task Time: 15 minutes

Preparation Time: Several hours

Resources: Examples of authentic British, North American, and local vocabulary; worksheet; answer key

PREAMBLE

This task should be used as a springboard to a discussion of attitudes toward different Englishes as well as a way of learning more English vocabulary. It can raise learners' consciousness about their expectations about and biases toward certain varieties of English.

WHAT THE TEACHER HAS TO DO

1. Select vocabulary from British, North American, and local sources that is different in form but carries the same meaning. Sources can include radio, television, videotapes, and print material.
2. Arrange the British and North American words in a table in either alphabetical or random order.
3. Leave the column for local equivalents blank for the learners to complete.
4. Prepare an answer key.

LEARNER PREPARATION

Encourage the learners, either in pairs or small groups, to discuss the different kinds of English they have heard. If you wish, stimulate the discussion by playing an audio- or videotape or by reading a text in one type of English. The interaction should develop into a discussion of "correct" or "real" English.

VARIATIONS

1. To make the task more challenging, include only one column of words in the table or randomly disperse the given words throughout the three columns.
2. Cut up and laminate the individual words and have learners match the British and American equivalents.
3. Adapt the task for a movie viewing. Have learners list various vocabulary differences and guess at the equivalents before viewing. During the film, have learners check their guesses. Cover local variations in a postviewing activity.

CONTRIBUTOR: Christine Heuring is a Language Instructor in the English Language Study-Center of Hong Kong Polytechnic University.

WORKSHEET

PREPARATION

Think about the differences between British English and American English vocabulary. Are there variations between the vocabulary in your local English and those varieties?

ACTIVITY

Write the local English word or words that are equivalent to the American and British ones in the table.

American English	British English	Local English
bus	coach	
check	tick	
crazy	mad	
drugstore	chemist('s)	
elevator	lift	
first floor	ground floor	
garbage	rubbish	
highway	motorway	
mail	post	
muffler (car)	silencer (car)	
railroad	railway	
restroom	public toilet	
round trip	return (ticket)	
sick	ill	
sidewalk	pavement	
store	shop	

Think about or discuss in pairs or groups your attitude or feelings about these vocabulary differences. Are some words considered to be "real" English or "correct" English? Are other words thought to be "incorrect" or "bad" English?

SELF-ASSESSMENT

Check your answers on the answer key. If you missed anything, consider the reasons why you did.

FURTHER SUGGESTION

Listen or read for more of these kinds of variations in vocabulary. Find out other people's attitudes toward these varieties of English.

What's the Acronym?

- [ ] beginner
- [ ] low intermediate
- [x] intermediate
- [ ] advanced

- [x] individual
- [x] pair
- [x] group
- [ ] tutor-assisted

- [ ] in class
- [x] out of class
- [x] self-access center

Aims: Discover the nature of acronyms and what they stand for

Task Time: 20–30 minutes

Preparation Time: Several hours

Resources: Local audio, video, or print material that has acronyms; worksheet; answer key

PREAMBLE

Acronyms are commonly used both in the media and the workplace. This task allows learners to discover for themselves what acronyms are and how they are used.

WHAT THE TEACHER HAS TO DO

1. Scan local print material or local radio or television programs for frequently or currently used acronyms.
2. Collect the acronyms and their meanings. Prepare a worksheet that incorporates the acronyms and a place for learners to write down the meanings.
3. Prepare an answer key.

LEARNER PREPARATION

1. Give the learners some print material that contains acronyms or have the learners listen to an audio or video clip, perhaps from the news, that contains acronyms.
2. Ask the learners to guess the meanings of the acronyms.
3. Ask the learners to consider if knowing the acronyms' meanings would aid their understanding or enjoyment of the material.

CONTRIBUTOR: Christine Heuring is a Language Instructor in the English Language Study-Center of Hong Kong Polytechnic University.

WORKSHEET

BEFORE YOU BEGIN

Think about the following questions before you begin this task:

1. In listening and reading material, have you occasionally seen a series of capital letters that form a "word"? Do you know what these words mean?
2. Must you know the meaning of these words to fully understand the passage?

ACTIVITY

By yourself, with a partner, or in a group look at the following list of acronyms. Write down what you think each one means.

Acronym	What you think it means
BBC	*British Broadcasting Corporation*
PRC	
USA	
RAM	
UN	
UCLA	
IBM	
GPO	
WTO	

SELF-ASSESSMENT

Check your answers with the answer key.

FURTHER SUGGESTIONS

1. Over the next week write down any acronyms you encounter. Try to find out their meanings before your next study session. Bring your findings for discussion.

2. Create your own acronyms. See if your group members, classmates, or instructor can guess their meanings. Make sure to provide a suitable context for your acronyms.

3. Keep a diary of acronyms that you come across. Note the acronyms that are in current use and those that are not. Their use may be directly related to newsworthy events.

Picture Matching

☑ beginner
☑ low intermediate
☐ intermediate
☐ advanced

☑ individual
☐ pair
☐ group
☐ tutor-assisted

☐ in class
☐ out of class
☑ self-access center

Aims: Identify objects and name them

Task Time: 20 minutes

Preparation Time: 15 minutes

Resources: Audiotape, audiotape recorder, picture cards, worksheet

PREAMBLE

This task is an enjoyable way to introduce new vocabulary and to determine an unknown object from its description. The use of picture cards helps learners remember the word by putting an image of the item in their memory.

WHAT THE TEACHER HAS TO DO

1. Make a set of picture cards with the identifying noun on the back (or use a commercially available set).
2. On an audiotape, record sounds or descriptions that can be used to identify the objects on the picture cards.
3. Record an ordered list of the names of the objects directly after the sounds and descriptions.
4. Note the counter numbers for the two recordings.

CONTRIBUTOR: Paul Kovács teaches EFL and English for specific purposes at International House in Huelva, Spain.

WORKSHEET

PREPARATION

For this worksheet you need Audiotape No. _____ and Picture Pack No. _____.

1. Make sure the audiotape is wound to Counter No. _____.
2. Place all the cards on the table with the pictures facing up.

ACTIVITY

1. Listen to Section 1 of the audiotape and select the picture that best fits the sound or description on the audiotape. Put the pictures into an ordered pile as you hear the sounds and descriptions. Continue listening to Section 1 until you have identified all the pictures.
2. After you have listened to the first part of the audiotape, turn the cards over one by one and look at the words on the back of the cards as you listen to Section 2 of the audiotape.
3. If you have any problems, listen again to Section 1 of the audiotape.

FURTHER SUGGESTION

Write one sentence for each new word you have learned and show the sentences to your teacher.

Vocabulary Development

Aims: Learn to increase vocabulary and correctly use newly acquired words independently

Task Time: 30 minutes

Preparation Time: 10 minutes

Resources: Bound notebook (or computer and disk), dictionary, English language newspaper, worksheet

PREAMBLE

This task enables learners to increase their vocabulary and ensures that their usage of the new vocabulary is correct. Most learners memorize only the meaning and part of speech of a particular unknown word and end up using an unfamiliar word in situations where it seems suitable. By studying the sample core phrases in this task, the learners are better able to recognize how words are commonly used. Recording this information in a notebook (or on a computer disk) provides the learners with personalized dictionaries of newly acquired words.

WHAT THE TEACHER HAS TO DO

1. Make blank copies of the sample worksheet.
2. Distribute the worksheet in class or put it in the vocabulary section of the self-access study center.

VARIATION

Once your learners have started collecting vocabulary in this way, have them bring their lists to class and share the new words with each other.

CONTRIBUTOR: Ron Lane is a lecturer in the Science and Technology Department at Keio University in Tokyo, Japan.

WORKSHEET

INSTRUCTIONS

1. Copy the word table below into your notebook or enter it onto your computer disk. A few sample entries are shown in the table; ignore these if you wish.
2. Read any article in an English language newspaper and underline or highlight any word whose meaning is either unknown or unclear to you.
3. Fill in the word table with the unknown words, their parts of speech, and their meanings. (Use your dictionary or work with a partner.) In the last column (sample core phrase), write a short phrase that includes the unknown word written in capital letters and one or two words occurring before and after the unknown word as it appears in the newspaper article.
4. Memorize the meaning of each word and become comfortable with its usage in the sample core phrase column.

Word	Meaning	Sample core phrase
devastation, n.	ruin	economic DEVASTATION caused the company to close
glaring, adj.	strong, unpleasant sunlight	the most GLARING example
lure, n.	attraction	the economic LURE is strong
[etc.]		

WORKSHEET

Using a Portable Electronic Dictionary: Finding the Right Definition

☐ beginner	
☐ low intermediate	
☑ intermediate	
☑ advanced	
☑ individual	
☐ pair	
☐ group	
☐ tutor-assisted	
☐ in class	
☑ out of class	
☑ self-access center	

Aims: Practice finding correct dictionary definitions

Task Time: 20–30 minutes

Preparation Time: 45–60 minutes

Resources: Portable electronic dictionary, worksheet, answer key

PREAMBLE

Portable electronic dictionaries are increasingly common in some parts of the world, and their quality is improving. They have some advantages over paper dictionaries, such as portability, ease of use, and (for some) speech, but one disadvantage is that only part of all but the shortest entries is visible on the screen at one time. Learners may thus tend to pick one of the first definitions they see as long as it appears to be moderately close to what they are looking for, rather than look through the whole entry. The manual that comes with the electronic dictionary may provide some help, but learners may easily overlook it. This task focuses learners' attention on this issue and gives practice in choosing the correct definition.

WHAT THE TEACHER HAS TO DO

1. Identify the situation: (a) Do the learners all use the same electronic dictionary, or do they use more than one model? (b) Are the dictionaries monolingual or bilingual? For this task, electronic dictionaries will preferably be provided in the self-access center, but learners may use their own.
2. Select suitable words for use in the worksheet, that is, words with several definitions (monolingual dictionaries) or equivalents (bilingual dictionaries). Appropriate words may involve more than one entry. That is, a pair of homonyms may be listed under two headwords, each given a number, such as *bank[1]* (*area beside a river*), and *bank[2]* (*place for storing something, especially money*). Some dictionaries have separate entries for different parts of speech, such as *brush* (n.) and *brush* (v.).
3. If more than one type of electronic dictionary is in use, select definitions that are unlikely to be given first in an entry. If only one dictionary is in use, work directly with it.
4. Prepare an answer key. If one type of dictionary is in use, give only the definition number (and headword number, if applicable). If the learners use more than one type of dictionary, give an actual definition or an equivalent (see the sample answer key).

VARIATION

Use this type of exercise for printed dictionaries. Finding the right definition is not as difficult, as learners can see a whole page at once, but they may still select definitions occurring early in an entry rather than checking the whole entry. This exercise may be of particular use in translation courses.

CONTRIBUTORS: Andrew Taylor is Associate Professor in the Department of English, and Adelaide Chan is a Senior Lecturer in the Division of Humanities and Social Sciences, both at the City University of Hong Kong.

ACTIVITY: FIND THE RIGHT DEFINITION*

In each of the sentences below one word is underlined. Look up each underlined word in a portable electronic dictionary and find the definition that fits best. Write it in the space provided.

Sentence	Definition of underlined word
1. The task was assigned to several <u>raw</u> recruits.	
2. She was very <u>short</u> with him when he arrived late.	
3. The drunken man <u>reeled</u> from side to side.	
4. She has a <u>passion</u> for fast cars.	
5. Due to the loss of our biggest customer, the company's financial situation is <u>grave</u>.	
6. The <u>net</u> result of the first year of trading is a profit of $20,000.	
7. I had a <u>brush</u> with her during the last meeting.	
8. When she was punished by the school principal, she was <u>cured</u> of skipping classes.	
9. He's quite a <u>character</u>.	
10. As your check <u>bounced</u>, we cannot accept another order from you.	

SAMPLE ANSWER KEY

The right definitions will be similar to the ones listed below. The part of speech has been included to help you check back to find the right definition in your dictionary if you need to. This is because some dictionaries have separate entries for each part of speech (e.g., *brush¹ n(oun)* and *brush² v(erb)*).

Part of speech	Definition
1. adjective	very new and untrained
2. adjective	rude and impatient, curt
3. verb	walk unsteadily, stagger
4. noun	very strong interest in something, a great liking for something
5. adjective	very serious
6. adjective	final, when there is nothing more to be subtracted
7. noun	a short, unfriendly argument or disagreement

*For this worksheet it is assumed that (a) the learners are using a variety of electronic dictionaries and (b) the dictionaries are monolingual.

Part of speech	Definition
8. verb	stop someone from behaving badly
9. noun	an interesting or unusual person
10. verb	be returned because there is not enough money in the account

Very often the right answer is not the first definition given in the dictionary. In fact, you may have to look at several screens before you find it. So check all of them. It doesn't take long! Sometimes you might not find any definition that fits the sentence well. The dictionary might not have included one. But in most cases you will find one, so it is worth making the effort to look.

Vocabulary for ...

Aims: Learn high-frequency vocabulary items relevant to professional and academic needs

Task Time: 30 minutes

Preparation Time: 2 hours

Resources: Professional journals, newspapers, textbooks, or texts written by learners, audiotape, audiotape player, worksheet, answer key

PREAMBLE

This task helps learners practice the vocabulary they need for both academic and professional purposes. An audiotape reinforces the target language, helps learners recognize both spoken and written forms, and can be used for oral practice.

WHAT THE TEACHER HAS TO DO

1. Identify an appropriate text. Texts written by learners often indicate the vocabulary for which they have an immediate need.
2. Make two copies of the text, A and B. On Copy A blank out the target vocabulary. Number the blanks for ease of reference. Leave Copy B intact.
3. Make a numbered answer key showing the missing words, acceptable alternatives, and explanations of meaning.
4. Record the passage on an audiotape. Note the counter numbers for the beginning of the recording.
5. Provide a short follow-up activity that requires the learner to use the vocabulary in a new context.

VARIATION

Prepare a series of worksheets based on the same text that meet the needs of the learners at various levels and that are specific to different departments, interests, or topics.

CONTRIBUTOR: Beverley Teague is a Lecturer in the Language Institute at the City University of Hong Kong.

WORKSHEET

PREPARATION

For this worksheet you need Audiotape No. _____.

BEFORE YOU BEGIN

1. Make sure the audiotape is rewound to the beginning.
2. Set the audiotape counter to 000.
3. Forward the audiotape. Stop the audiotape when the counter reaches _____.

ACTIVITY

1. Read the article that accompanies this worksheet.
2. Write a list of words to fill the gaps. Sometimes more than one word might be suitable.
3. Listen to the audiotape and read the article while you listen. As you listen, check your words.
4. Check your words against the answer key.
5. Record what you have done in your self-access diary.

SAMPLE ANSWER KEY

Missing word/ alternative words	Meaning
1. *cause/create/face*	*cause* and *create* put the focus on the cost to society; *face* suggests sympathy for the mother
2. *has given birth to*	If you are focusing attention on the baby: *the baby was born at 8:15 p.m.*
	If you are focusing attention on the mother: *the mother gave birth at 8:15 p.m.*
3. [etc.]	

CHAPTER 7

Grammar

Thinking about and improving the use of English grammar is the focus of a variety of tasks in this chapter. In the tasks learners check texts carefully, match ideas with concordance checklists, proofread passages, review materials used in class, and record examples of imperfect English. Through these activities learners discover more about the facts, rules, and choices involved in using grammar. Many of the tasks suggest that learners use good grammar reference books to help them understand more about grammar.

A Friend of Mine Has a Problem

Aims: Practice the forms used in giving advice

Task Time: 30 minutes

Preparation Time: 30 minutes

Resources: Written statements of a problem, worksheet

PREAMBLE

Advice giving is an area of language use that learners find interesting and hence that stimulates a lot of language use. Several forms can be used to begin an advice-giving exchange. This task provides relevant problems for learners to respond to and practice in the forms used in beginning an advice-giving exchange.

WHAT THE TEACHER HAS TO DO

1. Write a short but rather detailed description of a problem that is relevant to learners. Base the problem on your own experiences with the target culture, or collect problems from learners and edit them.
2. Attach the problem to a piece of paper, and place it in an envelope in the self-access center.
3. Invite responses to the problem.
4. Make the worksheet available to those who want to respond to the problem.
5. When responses have accumulated in the envelope, correct them and return them to the writers.

LEARNER PREPARATION

Before doing this task, give learners formal instruction with the language used for giving advice.

VARIATIONS

1. Ask learners to write up their own problems, the problems of a friend, or imaginary problems. Place them in separate envelopes.
2. Encourage respondents to ask questions for the original problem writer to respond to. This makes the task more communicative and involves clarification and negotiation of meaning.
3. For more advanced learners, use advice columns from the newspaper.

CONTRIBUTOR: Eric Bray teaches at Doshisha University and Doshisha Women's College in Japan.

WORKSHEET

YOUR TASK

1. Read the problem in the envelope and think about the writer's problem. Do you have any good advice to give him or her?
2. Write a paragraph or two in which you give this person some advice. Be sure to use some of the following expressions to begin your advice-giving sentences.

Form	Situation
He ought to + (base form of the verb)	authority or urgency
She had better + (base form of the verb)	authority or urgency
You should + (base form of the verb)	standard form
If I were you, I would + (base form of the verb)	friendly/not urgent
Why don't you + (base form of the verb)	friendly/not urgent
How about + (gerund)	friendly/not urgent

DO YOU KNOW THESE FORMS?

Are any of the advice-giving forms above new to you? If so, circle the new ones and try to use them when you write your advice. Remember that the guidelines given above are very general, and usage may vary depending on context.

Write your advice below:

WORKSHEET

Error Search

- [ ] beginner
- [ ] low intermediate
- [ ] intermediate
- [x] advanced

- [x] individual
- [ ] pair
- [ ] group
- [ ] tutor-assisted

- [ ] in class
- [x] out of class
- [ ] self-access center

Aims: Recognize "mistakes" that native speakers make; distinguish prescriptive and descriptive grammar

Task Time: One academic term

Preparation Time: 5 minutes

Resources: Worksheet

PREAMBLE

This task shows learners that native speakers of English do not always use English correctly and encourages learners of English not to be afraid to make mistakes.

WHAT THE TEACHER HAS TO DO

Adapt the worksheet to suit the needs of your learners and their learning context.

LEARNER PREPARATION

Teach a session on the differences between descriptive and prescriptive approaches to language.

VARIATIONS

1. Where learners do not have access to English being used in natural contexts, substitute video clips from current movies.
2. To use this task for assessment, tell learners they will receive one point for each different type of error they collect and correctly identify.

CONTRIBUTOR: Dennis Bricault is Director of ESL Programs and Instructor in Spanish at North Park College, Chicago, Illinois, in the United States.

WORKSHEET

PREPARATION

1. Do you speak your language perfectly?
2. Do all Britons, Australians, and North Americans speak perfect English?
3. Where do you think the best and worst English is spoken?

Languages are not always used according to what grammar books teach. In casual speech we tend to use language in a less controlled way. Some of the best places to listen to English spoken casually are

[List relevant local places.]

Don't expect to hear much casual speech on TV or radio because speakers are professionals who make relatively few mistakes.

ACTIVITY

For the rest of this academic term, keep a record of any "imperfect" English you hear. You may record either spoken or written samples. The samples must be from native speakers of English. Keep a notebook with records like the following:

Date	Source	Sample	Error
3/6/95	man on bus	That don't look right.	don't ➜ doesn't

Speculation

Aims: Learn and practice modal verbs used for speculating

Task Time: 15 minutes

Preparation Time: 15 minutes

Resources: Two photographs (or convincing drawings) of two people, one of a personality that learners will recognize and the other of an anonymous person; worksheet

PREAMBLE

This task helps learners recognize and contrast speech used to state facts and speculate about people.

WHAT THE TEACHER HAS TO DO

1. Choose appropriate photographs or drawings of two people. Magazine covers or newspaper photographs work well. The task is more effective if the photograph of the unknown person is humorous or dramatic; above all, it must invite speculation.
2. Add the photographs to Worksheet 2. Put the photograph of the famous person under the *Facts* heading and the photograph of the unknown person under the *Guesses* heading.

LEARNER PREPARATION

Review the use of modals.

VARIATION

Replace the photographs with video clips.

REFERENCE

Azar, B. (1989). *Understanding and using English grammar* (2nd ed.). Englewood Cliffs, NJ: Prentice Hall.

CONTRIBUTOR: Dennis Bricault is Director of ESL Programs and Instructor in Spanish at North Park College, Chicago, Illinois, in the United States.

Worksheet 1

PREPARATION

Familiarize yourself with the information in the following grammar chart (adapted from Azar, 1989, pp. 92, 95, 98).

Degree of certainty	Positive	Negative
About the present		
Fact (100% certain)	is	isn't
Deduction (95% certain)	must	must not
		couldn't
		can't
Guess (50% certain)	may	may not
	might	might not
	could	
About the past		
Fact (100% certain	was	wasn't
Deduction (95% certain)	must have	must not have
		couldn't have
		can't have
Guess (50% certain)	may have	may not have
	might have	might not have
	could have	

ACTIVITY

1. Look at the photographs on Worksheet 2 and complete as much as you can of the *Facts* section.

2. Make positive and negative guesses about the person in the *Guesses* section. Your guesses can be as wild as you like.

SELF-ASSESSMENT

Check your sentences against the grammar chart. Sentences you have written in the first box should correspond with facts in the chart. Sentences in the second box should correspond with deductions (from what you see) or guesses.

FURTHER SUGGESTION

Go with a friend to a public place. Observe two or three people. Write down what you know about them and what you guess about them in a *Facts* box and a *Guesses* box. Compare your sentences.

Worksheet 2

FACTS

[Paste photograph of known personality here.]

Name:

Age:

Job:

Marital status:

Country of origin:

Personality:

Likes:

Dislikes:

Other information:

GUESSES

[Paste photograph of unknown personality here.]

Name:

Age:

Job:

Marital status:

Country of origin:

Personality:

Likes:

Dislikes:

Other information:

Learning by Example

☐ beginner
☑ low intermediate
☑ intermediate
☑ advanced

☑ individual
☐ pair
☐ group
☑ tutor-assisted

☐ in class
☐ out of class
☑ self-access center

Aims: Use examples of good writing to improve the use of grammar

Task Time: Variable

Preparation Time: 5 minutes while marking assignments

Resources: Personal computer, concordancing software, corpus of good learner assignments, worksheet

PREAMBLE

This task encourages learners to use good examples of their peers' work to construct rules for overcoming their own errors. It also forms a bridge between the classroom and the self-access center. Once learners have mastered this technique, they may continue to use it without prompting from the teacher. This task can also familiarize learners with sentence structures and terminology that are specific to particular subject areas.

WHAT THE TEACHER HAS TO DO

1. Prepare an ASCII text file containing a number of good student assignments that have been corrected (i.e., that do not contain errors) for use with concordancing software (e.g., *Longman Mini-Concordance*r or *MicroConcord*).
2. Adapt the worksheet for your own needs.
3. The next time you are marking, using one copy of the worksheet for each learner, fill in the first box and ask the learners to complete the work in the self-access center (or wherever the concordancing software and corpus are available).

LEARNER PREPARATION

Hold a session on the value of a concordancer and how it works.

VARIATION

To adapt this task for use without the bridge between the classroom and the self-access center, provide error-ridden assignments with teacher's correction marks on them. Let learners use them for constructing their own rules.

REFERENCES

Longman mini-concordancer [Computer software]. (1989). Harlow, England: Longman.
Scott, M., & Johns, T. (1993). *MicroConcord* [Computer software]. Oxford: Oxford University Press.

CONTRIBUTOR: *David Gardner is a Senior Language Instructor in the English Center of the University of Hong Kong.*

Name: _____

You are using the following words incorrectly:

ACTIVITY

1. Go to the self-access center and use the *Longman Mini-Concordancer* software.
2. Select the Student Essay Corpus.
3. Use the New Word option (on the Concordance menu) with each of the words in the box above.
4. Compare the way(s) each word is used in the corpus with the way(s) you have used it.
5. From looking at the examples in the corpus, make rules for yourself about how to use the words. Below write your rules and write examples to support them:

Grammar Gap Filling

☐ beginner
☐ low intermediate
☑ intermediate
☑ advanced

☑ individual
☐ pair
☐ group
☐ tutor-assisted

☑ in class
☑ out of class
☑ self-access center

Aims: Practice grammar in an authentic context

Task Time: 20 minutes +

Preparation Time: 10 minutes

Resources: One or more newspaper articles, bottle of typist's correction fluid, worksheet

PREAMBLE

Single-sentence gap-filling exercises often either do not provide sufficient context for learners to make sensible choices or provide clues that make the exercise too simple. In addition, it is difficult to give the sentences in such exercises a feeling of authenticity, and writing such exercises is very time consuming. In contrast, this task gives the learner authentic texts with very little preparation on the part of the teacher.

WHAT THE TEACHER HAS TO DO

1. Select a newspaper article that suits the needs of your learners.
2. Make two copies of the article. (Note: In some countries it is necessary to obtain permission to copy newspaper articles. This is rarely denied.) Use a photocopier to enlarge them if possible. Label one *Article* and the other *Answer Key*.
3. Decide on the feature you want learners to practice (e.g., tenses, articles, adverbs).
4. On the answer key, underline the words in the article that you have chosen to highlight the feature.
5. On the copy labeled *Article,* use the correction fluid to blank out the relevant words and create the gap-filling exercise.
6. Number the gaps.
7. Attach the article (and the answer key) to the worksheet.

VARIATIONS

1. Use this exercise to practice different classes of words or a random selection of grammatical items.
2. Develop a series of worksheets that address different grammatical points (e.g,. prepositions, tenses, adjectives, noun-verb agreement) and that reflect different levels of difficulty.

CONTRIBUTOR: David Gardner is a Senior Language Instructor in the English Center of the University of Hong Kong.

ACTIVITY

In the attached newspaper article a number of words are missing. Work out from the text what the words should be and write them below.

1.	16.
2.	17.
3.	18.
4.	19.
5.	20.
6.	21.
7.	22.
8.	23.
9.	24.
10.	25.
11.	26.
12.	27.
13.	28.
14.	29.
15.	30.

HOW WELL DID YOU DO?

When you have finished, check your answers with the answer key. If your words and the ones on the answer key are different, use a dictionary to see if:

1. they have the same meaning
2. they are grammatically the same

Guess the Verbs

Aims: Learn verbs to use in a written text; consolidate a grammar point by thinking about textual clues

Task Time: Variable

Preparation Time: 15 minutes

Resources: Stories written by the teacher, or by the students in class

PREAMBLE

It is often difficult to know when students understand and can apply the grammar rules taught in class. This enjoyable task allows learners to practice grammar on their own and gives them a break from class-based exercises, which can be repetitive and boring.

WHAT THE TEACHER HAS TO DO

1. Collect a variety of short stories.
2. Decide on the grammar point to focus on: verbs, prepositions, articles, and so on.
3. Retype the story, inserting nonsense words for the words in the grammatical category you are focusing on. Use the nonsense words consistently—that is, use the same nonsense word (e.g., *freg*) to replace each occurrence of a word (e.g., *went*) in the text.
4. Make an answer key.

VARIATIONS

1. Adapt the task for different parts of speech: prepositions, articles, comparatives, conditionals, adverbs, and others.
2. Use this task after a grammar lesson in class. Then get your students to prepare similar stories with their own nonsense words (plus an answer key). Place these stories in the self-access center.

CONTRIBUTOR: Lindsay Miller is Assistant Professor in the English Department at City University of Hong Kong.

WORKSHEET

PREPARATION

1. What is a verb?
2. What types of verbs do you know?
3. Circle the verbs in the list below.

see	happy	tall	running	man	to go
verb	can	think	painting	as	special
because	cookie	have	leave		

Check your answer with the answer card. If you had any problems, look up the word in your dictionary to find the meaning and use of the word.

ACTIVITY

In the story that follows, the verbs have been replaced with nonsense words (words with no meaning) in boldface. Read the story and try to give a meaning to the nonsense words (e.g., *The boy wuk the ice cream.* = *The boy ate the ice cream.*).

Note: The verbs that are the same in the story are replaced by the same nonsense word, and the nonsense words are the same length as the verbs they replace.

Last week I **freg** to visit Andrew, a friend of mine. Andrew **az** in hospital with a broken leg. He **qik** crossing the street when a motorcyclist **dup** him. He was **kenta** to hospital, and because it **qik** a bad break the doctor **cidezew** to keep him in the hospital for a few days. He is **fubbert** very bored and **az** always happy to **tre** a friend for an hour or two!

I usually **kent** a bus to the hospital, but on my last visit I **cidezew** to **kent** a taxi. The taxi driver **freg** the wrong way, and I **qik** very late in **fubbert** to Andrew. Still, I **ter** him for half an hour and managed to cheer him up a bit. Next visit I will **kent** the bus again.

SELF-ASSESSMENT

1. Look at the answer key and see how well you did. Did you have any problems?
2. In your dictionary, check the meaning any verbs you could not guess. Look at the explanation of how to use the verbs in your grammar book. If you are still not sure, ask a teacher.

Proofreading

☑ beginner
☑ low intermediate
☑ intermediate
☑ advanced

☑ individual
☐ pair
☐ group
☐ tutor-assisted

☑ in class
☑ out of class
☑ self-access center

Aims: Correct grammar errors

Task Time: Variable

Preparation Time: 1 hour

Resources: Learners' written assignments, worksheet, answer key

PREAMBLE

For this task the teacher uses learners' assignments to make proofreading passages of varying lengths and difficulty that focus either on several grammatical items or on a single item. The task helps learners realize how grammatical items appear in context, how to correct their own errors, and how to use words correctly.

WHAT THE TEACHER HAS TO DO

1. Collect and photocopy learners' written assignments.
2. Choose an assignment. If the assignment is long, choose an extract from it suitable to the length and difficulty of the proofreading passage you intend to develop.
3. Revise and correct the grammar errors in the extract so that only one grammar error remains on each line (see the sample worksheet).
4. Type up the resulting proofreading passage.
5. Write an answer key to the proofreading passage.

CONTRIBUTOR: Alison Wong is a Lecturer in the Language Institute at the City University of Hong Kong.

WORKSHEET

ACTIVITY

In the passage below, *each line* contains *one* grammatical error.

- Underline each error and write the corrected version in the space provided.
- If a word is missing, mark its place with an arrow (↑) and write it in the space provided.
- If a word does not belong, cross out the word and write it down in the space provided.

It is a good idea to refer to a grammar reference book while you do this activity.

When I was child, I had an accident in a very crowded street.	1. _____
What is the accident? My small hand was hurt by a lit cigarette.	2. _____
It was a really unhappy experience and it makes me aware of	3. _____
dangers of smoking. Today, I have the view that banning cigarette	4. _____
smoking at public places is the correct thing to do. Even the	5. _____

Grammar

Legislative Council establishes a law that prohibits smoking in   6.＿＿＿＿＿＿
public places, such as cinema. The public areas should be   7.＿＿＿＿＿＿
demark for smoking or nonsmoking.   8.＿＿＿＿＿＿

ANSWER KEY

When I was ↑ child, I had an accident in a very crowded street.   1. a
What <u>is</u> the accident? My small hand was hurt by a lit cigarette.   2. was
It was a really unhappy experience and it <u>makes</u> me aware of   3. made
↑ dangers of smoking. Today, I have the view that banning cigarette   4. the
smoking <u>at</u> public places is the correct thing to do. Even the   5. in
Legislative Council <u>establishes</u> a law that prohibits smoking in   6. has established
public places, such as <u>cinema</u>. The public areas should be   7. cinemas
<u>demark</u> for smoking or nonsmoking.   8. marked

Now check a good grammar reference book to understand the corrections.

Understanding the Nature of Grammar

- [ ] beginner
- [ ] low intermediate
- [x] intermediate
- [ ] advanced

- [x] individual
- [ ] pair
- [ ] group
- [ ] tutor-assisted

- [ ] in class
- [x] out of class
- [x] self-access center

Aims: Understand the nature of grammar and ways to improve the use of it

Task Time: 30 minutes

Preparation Time: 5 minutes

Resources: Worksheet, answer key

PREAMBLE

Problems with grammar can cause a lack of fluency at best and communication breakdown at worst. The self-access center is an ideal place for learners to work on their specific problems at their own pace, and the first important step is for them to understand the nature of grammar and the best ways to approach it.

WHAT THE TEACHER HAS TO DO

1. Adapt the worksheet to suit the needs of your learners.
2. Write an answer key.

VARIATION

Encourage learners to use the informational worksheet in conjunction with grammar exercise worksheets.

CONTRIBUTOR: Mabel C. P. Wong is a freelance ESL specialist in Victoria, Australia.

WORKSHEET

What Is Grammar?

The term *grammar* is so broad that it is concerned with everything related to a language. The following diagram shows that the grammar of English can be divided into three main areas.

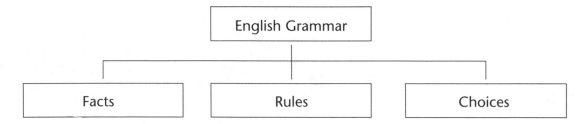

FACTS

This part of grammar cannot be applied generally. For example, the plural form of *man* is *men*, not *mans*; the past tense of *go* is *went*; and so on.

RULES

When we say something, we do not throw words together at random. There are rules monitoring the combination of words. This part of grammar shows how a language falls into certain patterns. Once the rules are learned, they can be used to create entirely original sentences. For instance, you can easily use the structure in the sentence *What do you think?* to formulate a large number of new sentences grammatically, for instance, *What did you see? What does he want?* and so forth.

CHOICES

In any situation you may have a choice of language forms that are all grammatically correct. This choice may be completely free. For example, you may choose between *Could you please tell me ...* and *Have you any idea about ...* while your intended meaning remains unchanged. However, you may sometimes use a different variety of English on purpose when the situation, the audience, the formality level, and your intention change. For example, you sound more irritated when you say "My roommate's always losing his keys" than when you say "My roommate always loses his keys." The differences in meaning caused by different varieties can sometimes be so subtle that you need to develop a deeper understanding of how meaning and grammar are related.

What are the most effective ways of learning grammar within the three categories? Write your answers below.

Facts

Rules

Choices

Check your answers on the answer key.

ANSWER KEY

What Is Grammar?

Facts: The only way to become familiar with facts is to learn them. You have to accept the facts for what they are rather than waste time worrying about them or challenging them. It is important that you take on the responsibility for learning these in your own time.

Rules: They need to be discovered. There are some consistent patterns in English. Once you have observed a pattern, you should be prepared to experiment by using it to create new sentences. If the rule works for them as well, your guess is probably a good one. If not, you will have to modify it or replace it with a better rule. This procedure involves some trial and error, but later when you become familiar with some rules, you can generate new language from them freely. Even though you know a limited number of words, you can put them together in an unlimited variety of ways. This type of exercise is confidence-boosting and motivating because it saves you time and effort. You can experiment with rules either on your own, in pairs, or in groups so that the activity can be more interesting, meaningful, and communicative.

Choices: You might think that for each situation only one single expression or sentence structure is correct. In fact, the use of certain grammatical forms is a matter of personal choice. It certainly takes a long time and a lot of exposure to the target language before you can develop a deep understanding of the relationship between grammar and meaning and its subtle distinctions. You should read and listen to English as much as possible for examples of grammar in context. The more you read and listen to English, the easier it will become.

MATERIALS FOR GRAMMAR

To improve your grammar, you need the help of grammar books. It is important to choose a grammar book that suits you. If you have found a suitable one, ask yourself these questions:

- Is the index easy to follow?
- Are the explanations simple and clear enough?
- Are there enough details?
- Is the language up-to-date?

If the answers are *no*, look at another book. You should feel free to add more criteria. For example, you may want exercises and answer keys in addition to explanations.

WAYS OF ORGANIZING YOUR GRAMMAR LEARNING

1. Set a regular time for practicing grammar.
2. Get a grammar book you find easy to use.
3. Keep a log book that notes points you have learned and rules you are testing.
4. Review regularly what you have learned.
5. Listen to and read English as much as possible.
6. Join discussion groups to try out new grammar points.
7. Make appointments with consultants and teachers to discuss grammatical problems.

Finally, do not be obsessed with being correct all the time. More important, do not assume that you should wait until you have mastered "perfect grammar" before you use the language. Keep practicing, and it may surprise you how fast you improve.

Paralinguistics

Language is more than words, and asking learners to stop and think about how they are communicating as well as what they are communicating is vital to overall communication strategies. The tasks in this chapter encourage learners to explore how their behavior can affect the messages they are trying to convey. Learners carefully examine gestures and body language to see if they are the same as those in their own culture. In many of the tasks learners watch videotapes and then role play, using paralinguistic features to enhance their communication.

The Effect of Good and Bad Behavior

- [ ] beginner
- [ ] low intermediate
- [x] intermediate
- [ ] advanced

- [ ] individual
- [x] pair
- [x] group
- [ ] tutor-assisted

- [ ] in class
- [ ] out of class
- [x] self-access center

Aims: Learn how to use behavior to help a situation

Task Time: 1 hour

Preparation Time: 30 minutes

Resources: Videotape containing examples of daily interaction, videotape player, worksheet, answer key

PREAMBLE

Behavior can help express meaning or it can confuse and cause problems in communicating in the target language. This task helps learners think about the effect behavior has on other people and to realize what a powerful weapon behavior can be.

WHAT THE TEACHER HAS TO DO

1. Select a segment of a videotape (up to half an hour in length) that contains examples of people dealing with each other on a day-to-day basis, such as in a shop, office, airport, or bank, and that shows the good or bad effects of behavior on people.
2. Note the counter number for the beginning of the segment on the worksheet.
3. Prepare an answer key.

VARIATIONS

1. Have learners perform contextualized role plays, making notes on the body language and its effect on the situation.
2. Have learners look out for examples of good and bad behavior and its effect in their day-to-day life.

CONTRIBUTOR: Sue Fitzgerald is an Instructor in the English Language Study-Center of Hong Kong Polytechnic University.

WORKSHEET

PREPARATION

For this worksheet you need to work with a partner or a group.
1. You need Videotape No. _____.
2. Rewind the videotape to the beginning.
3. Set the counter to 000. Then wind forward to Counter No. _____.

ACTIVITY

1. Watch the videotape all the way through. Make a note of what the characters in the film do and the effect their behavior has on the situation. As you watch, complete the following table *except* for the third column.

People	How do they behave?	What happens because of this behavior?	How could the person have behaved differently?

2. In pairs or groups discuss your answers.

3. Complete the last column.

4. Check your answers with the answer key. You may want to watch the videotape or certain parts of it again.

FURTHER SUGGESTIONS

1. Have each person in the group choose one of the characters from the videotape and role play the part. Videotape the role play if possible. The videotape could be used by other learners.

2. With a partner, role play a short scene. Ask the other members of your group to decide whether your behavior is acceptable or not.

3. Plan a weekly diary and make notes each day of how the people you meet act. At the end of each week, meet with your friends to discuss your notes.

What Does the Gesture Mean?

☑ beginner
☑ low intermediate
☑ intermediate
☑ advanced

☑ individual
☑ pair
☑ group
☐ tutor-assisted

☑ in class
☑ out of class
☑ self-access center

Aims: Become aware that the way people use their bodies gives various messages to other people

Task Time: 20 minutes

Preparation Time: 20 minutes

Resources: Pictures or drawings of people using gestures, answer key

PREAMBLE

This task helps learners understand what gestures mean and how to use them appropriately to convey meaning.

WHAT THE TEACHER HAS TO DO

1. Find some pictures or drawings of people using the gestures you want learners to learn.
2. On separate cards write out the meanings for those gestures, so that there are two cards for each gesture, one with the picture and one with the correct meaning for the gesture.
3. Prepare an answer key matching the gesture with its correct meaning.
4. Adapt the worksheet to suit the needs of your learners.

VARIATIONS

1. Group sets of pictures to focus on different kinds of nonverbal communication.
2. For groups, have each learner take a picture card without showing the others the picture. Learners then act out their gesture while the others try to guess what the gesture means. Write the answer at the bottom of the picture in case the actor does not know the meaning.
3. For groups of at least four learners, attach each picture card to its corresponding meaning card. Have the group split into two subgroups, A and B, and divide up the sets of cards without looking at them. Have each person in Group A except for one make up another meaning for one picture. Then have Group A members show the picture without the answer to Group B and give their meanings one at a time. The members of Group B have to decide who is giving the correct meaning. If they choose the wrong person, Group A wins points.

CONTRIBUTOR: Sue Fitzgerald is an Instructor in the English Language Study-Center of Hong Kong Polytechnic University.

WORKSHEET

PREPARATION

Collect the pictures and meanings from the appropriate envelope.

BEFORE YOU BEGIN

Think about the following questions.

1. The way you use your body sends various messages to other people, as in the example below. How do you use your body to express what you are saying (e.g,. hand movements, facial expressions)?

Gestures

We often use this gesture to wish ourselves luck in something.

2. People from different countries use the same gesture with different meanings. Can you think of any examples? What misunderstandings could arise from this?

ACTIVITY

1. Individually or as a group, match each picture of a gesture with the card containing its meaning.
2. When everyone in the group agrees on the matches, check your answers on the answer key.
3. Find out which gestures you and the members of your group have seen before and in which situations they were used.

FURTHER SUGGESTIONS

Here are some suggestions for practicing the gestures once you are familiar with them.

1. With one or more partners, prepare and act out a dialogue using as naturally as possible *all* the gestures you have learned.
2. In small groups, prepare a short role play including one or two of the gestures. The other members of the group try to guess which gesture you are using.

Identify the Gesture

Aims: Think about the paralinguistic features of communication

Task Time: 25 minutes

Preparation Time: 20 minutes

Resources: Videotape containing examples of paralinguistic gestures, videotape player, worksheet, answer key

PREAMBLE

Although knowledge of gestures does not replace competence in a language, it can help with communication if used effectively. When learners find themselves in situations where their oral communication is pushed to its limits, they can support communication by using gestures correctly. They can also cause a communication breakdown by using them wrongly. This task helps learners look for communicative gestures in the target language and decide whether they are the same as or different from those used in their native language.

WHAT THE TEACHER HAS TO DO

1. Select an appropriate videotape. It could be a film, an instructional videotape, or something you make yourself.
2. Look for a segment of approximately 3 minutes containing a gesture or gestures that you want learners to learn about.
3. Note the counter number for the beginning of the segment on the worksheet.
4. Write an answer key for the gestures.

VARIATIONS

1. Using one or more videotapes, build up a series of worksheets on gestures that are important for the learners to know.
2. Have learners work on the gestures in pairs.

CONTRIBUTOR: David Gardner is a Senior Language Instructor in the English Center of the University of Hong Kong.

WORKSHEET

PREPARATION

1. For this worksheet you need Videotape No. _____ .
2. Make sure the videotape is rewound to the beginning.
3. Set the counter to 000.
4. Wind the videotape to Counter Number _____.
5. Turn off the sound.

ACTIVITY

1. Watch (but do not listen to) about 3 minutes of the videotape. Each time someone makes a gesture (e.g., with hands, head, body) stop the videotape and add information to the first two columns of the following table.

Description of the gesture	What it means	Same or different in your language?

2. Watch the videotape again with the sound. Make changes in the table if you want.
3. Which of the gestures are the same in your own language, and which are different (Column 3)?
4. Check your answers with those on the answer key. If you missed anything, go back and look at the videotape again.

SAMPLE ANSWER KEY

Description of the gesture	What it means	Same or different in your language?
pointing at nose	referring to nose	different ("me")
pointing at a person	"you"	different (rude)
raising eyebrows	surprise	same
[etc.]		

Observing and Judging

☐ beginner
☐ low intermediate
☑ intermediate
☑ advanced

☐ individual
☑ pair
☑ group
☐ tutor-assisted

☑ in class
☐ out of class
☑ self-access center

Aims: Differentiate in making statements based on observation and those based on judgment

Task Time: 50 minutes

Preparation Time: 25 minutes

Resources: Photographs of people from magazines or newspapers, worksheet, answer key

PREAMBLE

When people look at cultural differences, they tend to judge them as if they were in their native country with people from their own culture and to make hasty judgments about such differences. These quick judgments are sometimes based on a lack of cultural information that is necessary for true understanding. This task shows how observing and asking about cultural differences in a nonjudgmental way can lead to a better understanding of aspects of culture that are often obscure.

WHAT THE TEACHER HAS TO DO

1. From newspapers or magazines, collect photographs containing people from a wide variety of cultures in different settings.
2. Paste each photograph onto a piece of card. This collection may be worth mounting for later use with other activities.
3. Number the photographs.
4. Prepare an answer key for Activity 1.

LEARNER PREPARATION

Hold a session on cultural differences.

VARIATION

Instead of using photographs or pictures, present a role play or a pantomime.

CONTRIBUTOR: Esther Kuntjara is an EFL instructor at Petra Christian University in Surabaya, Indonesia.

WORKSHEET

PREPARATION

You need to find a partner or a group to work with in order to use this worksheet.

BEFORE YOU BEGIN

Discuss these questions with a partner or in your group:

1. How do people in your country react to foreigners who have different behavior than they do? Do people generally accept differences, or do they expect foreign people to behave the same way they do?

2. How do people in your country react to someone who acts differently because of spending a lot of time with people from another culture?

ACTIVITY 1

There is a difference between observation and judgment. An observation is something we see, hear, or know to be true. A judgment is a personal opinion on what we see or hear. For example:

Observation: The man and the woman are hugging each other.
Judgment: It is shameful for a woman to hug a man in front of other people.

Decide together which of the following are observations and which are judgments:

1. He sighed and looked tired.
2. She is talking loudly because she is angry.
3. Rita is very superficial. She smiles too much.
4. I have not received a thank-you note from him.
5. He does not want to be friends with me.

Check your answers against the answer key.

ACTIVITY 2

For each of the photographs that accompany this worksheet, first make an observation and then a judgment that is appropriate in your own culture. Check each others' answers.

WHAT DID YOU LEARN?

1. Why is it important to distinguish between observing and judging?
2. How can this exercise be useful in learning a language?

FURTHER SUGGESTION

Arrange a role play that demonstrates the difference between observing and judging. Perform the role play for other people or for your own satisfaction.

Conveying and Interpreting Meaning

Aims: Interpret and convey meaning through gestures and body language

Task Time: 50 minutes

Preparation Time: 10 minutes

Resources: Worksheet

PREAMBLE

This task helps shy learners become less inhibited as they overcome their initial fear of making mistakes or not being understood. They also learn to appreciate how different people use different techniques and strategies when trying to communicate through nonverbal clues.

WHAT THE TEACHER HAS TO DO

Adapt the worksheet to suit the needs of your learners.

VARIATION

Change the situation on the worksheet to explore other nonverbal clues.

CONTRIBUTOR: Carmen F. Santás is a teacher in the secondary school Antón Fraguas de Fontiñas and a teacher trainer in the Institute of Education of the University of Santiago de Compostela, Spain.

WORKSHEET

PREPARATION

You need a group of four people to use this worksheet. Split into two pairs to do the activity below.

ACTIVITY

1. Each pair writes a very short dialogue for the situation given below:

   Two students are waiting at a bus stop. One explains a problem, and the other offers a solution to the problem.

2. Each pair *mimes* their dialogue (i.e., performs it without words). The other pair completes the table below while watching.

Body language (write a description):

Problem they described: Solution they described:

3. Each pair acts out their dialogue with words. The other pair completes the table below while watching and listening.

The real problem they described:

The real solution they described:

4. Once both pairs have finished, check that you have understood the problem and the solution correctly.

FURTHER SUGGESTION

Repeat this activity, today or another day, using a situation you think of yourselves.

Understanding a Key Scene in a Film

Aims: Interpret visual information and create a dialogue

Task Time: 1 hour

Preparation Time: 1 hour

Resources: Film on laser disc, laser disc player, caption decoder, worksheet, answer key

PREAMBLE

This task encourages learners to think of communication in its broadest sense. It helps them extract information from a text and interpret it in order to create a dialogue. Writing a dialogue encourages learners to interact with visual information, and the dialogue then becomes a useful resource for comparison with the original dialogue.

WHAT THE TEACHER HAS TO DO

1. Select a film on laser disc (look for a film with a theme that learners can relate to). You can use a film on videotape, but cuing the videotape and preparing a transcript will require time.
2. Select a chapter that will help learners understand the key elements in the film.
3. Add the film title and the selected chapter number to the worksheet.
4. Prepare an answer key.

VARIATION

Develop worksheets for key scenes in a film. On the worksheets, use charts to help learners extract information at deeper levels and develop greater sensitivity to language use.

CONTRIBUTOR: Beverley Teague is a Lecturer in the Language Institute at the City University of Hong Kong.

WORKSHEET

PREPARATION

1. You can work individually or with a friend. It is useful to be able to discuss your ideas with a friend.
2. Collect a laser disc. Go to a laser disc player with a caption decoder.
3. Make sure *sound* and *caption decoder* are both *off*.

ACTIVITY

1. Select Chapter _____. As you watch the chapter, write down the following for each person you see: name, sex, age, description, and role or relationship.
2. What is the chapter about? Write a short explanation (about 20 words).
3. Watch the chapter again (still with no sound) and write down what you imagine the people are saying. Watch more than once if you want.

4. If you are working with a friend, compare your dialogues when you have finished.

5. Now watch the film with *sound on* and *caption decoder on*. Compare your dialogue with what the people actually say.

HOW WELL DID YOU DO?

1. How close is your dialogue to the original?

2. Which of the following best describes your dialogue?
   - Totally different language and meaning
   - Different language but the same meaning
   - Language and meaning almost the same

CHAPTER 9

Self-Assessment

The self-assessment tasks encourage learners to take on the traditional role of the teacher as assessor of language abilities. Learners reflect on and examine their oral skills, reading, grammar, and writing, and checklists in the tasks stimulate thought and provide feedback without the need to depend on the teacher.

Test Score Evaluation

Aims: Receive feedback and follow-up guidelines after both successful and less successful test results

Task Time: 20 minutes

Preparation Time: Variable

Resources: Learners' test results, worksheet

PREAMBLE

This task reinforces immediate feedback that is encouraging and constructive. Completing the worksheet makes the learners form a more positive judgment of their language ability.

WHAT THE TEACHER HAS TO DO

1. Study the items of the test the learners wish to work on.
2. Divide the possible results into bands. The number of bands depends on the highest possible mark on the test. For a test with a total of 20 points, the bands could be 0–5, 6–11, 12–16, and 17–20.
3. Write an evaluation explaining what a score in each band means and offering some advice as to what a learner who earned a score in that band should do next. For each band, also direct learners to exercises, books, video- and audiotapes, and other self-access center materials.

CONTRIBUTOR: Isabelle Gore is a Lecturer in the Language Institute at the City University of Hong Kong.

WORKSHEET

Low Intermediate Listening Evaluation

PREPARATION

This worksheet is intended for use after you have completed a listening test.

ACTIVITY

1. Record the results of your listening test here: _____ /20.
2. Look below for an evaluation of your results.

Score = 16–20

If you have this score, you have done very well. It is time for you to get into a more challenging level that will also be more interesting for you.

Comments: Look at the intermediate section of the self-access center listening material. Look at Audiotape No. _____ and Task Sheet No. _____ to start with. You can also look at the videotapes at the intermediate level. Try Videotape No. _____ and Task Sheet No. _____ to start with. If you find these tasks too challenging, go to the preintermediate tasks on remedial work.

Score = 12–15

[Write an appropriate description and comments.]

Score = 7–11

[Write an appropriate description and comments.]

Score = 0–6

If you have this score, you have probably been working on tasks that are too challenging. You should try something simpler to begin with.

Comments: Look at the tasks in the low intermediate section of the self-access center. Look at the video- and audiotapes with pink labels and choose a topic of your choice. Then get the worksheets with the same code numbers as the tapes. All the video- and audiotapes with pink labels are probably more appropriate for you, and you will find you progress much faster when you use them.

Identifying Your Writing Difficulties

□ beginner
□ low intermediate
☑ intermediate
☑ advanced

☑ individual
□ pair
□ group
□ tutor-assisted

□ in class
☑ out of class
□ self-access center

Aims: Identify problems in writing; plan an appropriate self-study program

Task Time: Variable

Preparation Time: Variable

Resources: Worksheet

PREAMBLE

Learners who experience various difficulties in writing may find it hard to articulate exactly where the problems are. Even if they can vaguely locate their inadequacies, they may not know how to approach them. Similarly, many learners lack direction when they want to start a self-study program to improve their writing skills. This task helps them identify their writing needs and problems and thus formulate an effective self-study program tailored to their needs.

WHAT THE TEACHER HAS TO DO

Adapt the activities in the worksheet to suit your learners.

CONTRIBUTOR: Edward S. L. Li is a Senior Language Instructor in the Language Center of Hong Kong University of Science and Technology.

WORKSHEET

BEFORE YOU BEGIN

Take out your past writing assignments or essays. Check the errors your teachers highlighted and read the comments given carefully. What are the problems or errors that commonly occur in your writing?

ACTIVITY 1: TASK ANALYSIS

First, do you always know why you are writing, whom you are writing to, and how to express yourself to achieve your goal? Check the appropriate box below to see if you analyze a task vigorously enough before writing.

	Never	Sometimes	Always
1. Do you know what you want to achieve each time you write?	□	□	□
2. Do you know what the readers anticipate?	□	□	□
3. Do you write with the readers and their needs and expectations in mind?	□	□	□
4. Do you know what format and style are required for and appropriate to the writing task before you start?	□	□	□
5. Do you gather enough background knowledge to write on the given topic?	□	□	□

Very often, poor or ineffective writing is a result of inadequate analysis of the writing task. General problems that poor writers encounter include

- Not knowing what is to be achieved, resulting in writing that lacks direction and focus
- Not knowing what the readers know already or expect and thus failing to sustain interest or establish rapport and achieve effectiveness
- Writing in an inappropriate tone and style, which may come across to the readers as carelessness, immaturity, or, even worse, rudeness
- Not having done enough research to collect materials to write, resulting in writing that lacks substance. Thorough planning, however time consuming, is never a waste of energy. In fact, if you want your writing to be effective, planning is essential.

ACTIVITY 2: GRAMMAR AND VOCABULARY

Grammar and vocabulary are the tools you use to express your ideas and achieve your purpose, that is, to describe, explain, persuade, and so on. These important components of writing proficiency include the following:

- Correct use of tenses, articles, sentence structures, and other elements
- Appropriate choice of words and expressions
- Correct use of punctuation
- Correct spelling

Look at your past assignments, compositions, or essays. What are the usual teacher comments regarding grammar and vocabulary? Are you satisfied with your own performance in the following aspects?

Aspect	Not satisfied (lots of mistakes)	Satisfied (some mistakes)	Very satisfied (almost no mistakes)
1. Use of tenses/voices	☐	☐	☐
2. Use of articles	☐	☐	☐
3. Use of prepositions/phrasal verbs	☐	☐	☐
4. Use of sentence structures	☐	☐	☐
5. Use of connectives	☐	☐	☐
6. Use of punctuation	☐	☐	☐
7. Choice of vocabulary	☐	☐	☐
8. Choice of expressions	☐	☐	☐
9. Spelling	☐	☐	☐

Rating your performance in grammar and vocabulary helps you focus further on the source of your writing problems. It might turn out that your writing problems are actually related to your

- Limited vocabulary
- Inability to choose appropriate words and expressions for the context
- Poor command of grammar

If that is the case, you would profit by looking more closely at your needs in grammar and vocabulary.

ACTIVITY 3: TEXTUAL ORGANIZATION

A text should be organized cohesively and coherently. Some common problems in organization include the following:

- The ideas are not relevant or related.
- The ideas are presented in an arbitrary or ineffective order.
- The facts and evidence provided fail to support or establish the arguments or viewpoints.
- The main idea(s) is (are) not duly elaborated whereas the supportive ideas are given too much emphasis.

Have you had such comments on your written work before? Collect five of your written assignments or essays and read them carefully. Use the *four* criteria of good organization given in the box to evaluate your own writing. Grade your performance using the following scale:

| 1 = Poor (criterion not met) | 2 = OK (criterion partly met) | 3 = Very good (criterion fully met) |

Criterion	Text 1	Text 2	Text 3	Text 4	Text 5
1. *Development*: Ideas are relevant and presented to give a sense of direction and focus.					
2. *Continuity*: Facts and evidence given are consistent and supportive of the writer's point of view. Previously mentioned ideas are well related to newly introduced ones.					
3. *Balance*: Appropriate emphasis is given to each idea or point (main and supportive).					
4. *Completeness*: The topic/theme is discussed thoroughly from a number of perspectives.					

The next time you write, check to see whether your essay follows these four organizational principles.

ACTIVITY 4: WRITING STRATEGIES

Writing is not a *linear* process. Rather, it is a constant interaction between idea generation, style and word shaping, and mechanical revision. Skilled writers resort to various writing strategies to tackle their writing tasks. Check to see whether you adopt the same strategies when you write. Write *never, sometimes,* or *always* in the last column below.

Stage in the writing process	Writing strategies	Do you do this?
Planning	1. Spend time analyzing the purpose of the task, the readers, and the appropriate style required. Look for examples if necessary.	1.
	2. Generate ideas by brainstorming, reading, discussing, and interviewing people.	2.
	3. Gather information by reading relevant materials from all sources, such as journals, newspapers, and books.	3.
	4. Pool the information and ideas collected.	4.
Drafting and writing	5. Organize the information into several main points.	5.
	6. Get ideas onto paper quickly.	6.
	7. Concentrate on meaning rather than on grammatical accuracy.	7.
Revising and editing	8. Check the logic and balance of ideas.	8.
	9. Reorganize the ideas to establish coherence.	9.
	10. Check the effectiveness of paragraphing.	10.
	11. Revise at *all* levels—word, sentence, and textual.	11.
	12. Use the revision process to flesh out existing ideas by adding details or generating new content.	12.
	13. Distance yourself from the text for a couple of days.	13.
	14. Keep in mind the goals and the readers.	14.
	15. Make sure what you write is consistent with the objective.	15.
	16. Check grammar, spelling, punctuation, and vocabulary.	16.
	17. Check formality, style, and tone.	17.

Try these out the next time you write to see if you can write better. Of course, what works best for others may not be suitable for you, so be prepared to modify the strategies to suit your needs.

ACTIVITY 5: SUMMING UP

The answers to the questions in the previous activities helped you identify the problems that often affect your writing. Now form a profile of your writing needs. Begin with the areas in which you would like to see improvement.

PERSONAL WRITING NEEDS PROFILE

Writing needs	Areas I want to improve	Improvements I want to achieve
1.		
2.		
3.		
4.		

Self-Assessment

The profile can be a list of procedures to check your weak spots in your writing. It can be a list of strategies that you find useful in improving the quality of your work. (Refer to the good-writer strategies in Activity 4 for ideas.) Or it can be a list of language points for self-editing. If you want to target the writing demands in your study or work more specifically, ask yourself the following questions:

- What type of writing do I need most in my study or work?
- What type(s) of text do I find most difficult to write?
- What do I want to achieve on completion of the program?

With the answers to these questions and your needs profile in mind, set out to plan your self-study project. Keep a record of your work to check improvement. Alternatively, work with a friend and evaluate each other's work. You will be surprised at how much your friend is able to help. Also talk to the consultant if you need further advice.

Awareness Training

- [ ] beginner
- [x] low intermediate
- [x] intermediate
- [x] advanced

- [x] individual
- [ ] pair
- [x] group
- [ ] tutor-assisted

- [x] in class
- [x] out of class
- [ ] self-access center

Aims: Become aware of English and non-English language habits; generate ideas to change bad habits

Task Time: 2 weeks +

Preparation Time: Variable

Resources: Worksheets, monthly calendar for follow-up activity

PREAMBLE

In an ESL setting, many learners tend to mix with people speaking their native language outside the classroom and speak English only when they are in their English classes. As a result, these learners do not improve as much as they should. In an EFL setting, very few learners have the opportunity to meet native English speakers. Even when English written, audio, or video materials are available, learners may not take advantage of them. This task addresses these problems by asking learners to evaluate and plan to improve their language habits.

WHAT THE TEACHER HAS TO DO

1. Adapt the worksheets.
2. Have the learners complete Worksheet 1 in class or as an outside assignment.
3. In class, ask learners to find patterns in their language use and mark the habits they would like to change.
4. Have the learners find classmates who have similar goals. In small groups, have them generate a list of ways to change their language habits. Encourage them to think of resources available to them.
5. Have each group turn in the list. Consolidate the lists to form Worksheet 2.
6. During another class period, distribute Worksheet 2 and ask the groups to explain the suggestions they wrote as the class goes through the list.
7. Ask learners to identify the categories that apply to them (recommended: not more than three categories) and mark at least three activities that they would like to do to change their pattern.
8. Distribute Worksheet 3. Encourage learners to write concrete activities they plan to do to change their learning habits. Have the learners give you a copy of their contract.
9. At the beginning of the contract period at least, check that learners are doing what they said they were going to do.

VARIATION

Vary the items on the first worksheet or focus them on a specific skill area or learning strategy depending on their applicability to your learners.

CONTRIBUTOR: Ditte Lokon teaches at San Jose State University, California, in the United States.

Worksheet 1

Self-Monitoring Your Language Use

Name: _____ Period covered (dates): _____

Every evening before going to bed, fill out the table below with the number of hours you spent doing these activities. Do not spend more than 10 minutes per night filling this out.

Activity	Mon.	Tues.	Wed.	Thurs.	Fri.	Sat.	Sun.
Speaking/Listening							
Speak English with people from other countries (not in class)							
Speak English in class							
Speak English with Americans							
Speak your native language (not in class)							
Speak your native language in class							
Watch English TV/movies							
Watch programs in your native language							
Reading							
English materials (not including textbooks)							
Materials in your native language							
Studying							
Do homework/prepare for classes							
Sleeping							

Comments:

Worksheet 2

Ways to Change Your Language Habits

Below are some possible ways to increase or reduce the number of minutes or hours you spend on a particular activity. For each category that applies to you, put a check mark (✔) next to at least three activities that you would like to do.

TO MEET PEOPLE FROM OTHER COUNTRIES

- Go to bars.
- Go out alone.
- Go to coffee shops on weekends.
- Join a sports team.
- Talk to people I meet on the street.
- Go to discos.
- Smile more.
- Make jokes.
- Contact neighbors.
- Have a party; go to parties.
- Talk to friends' host families.
- Be more open when meeting new people.
- Go to the beach and talk to other beach goers.
- Play volleyball at the beach (other people might come and join).
- Join other people playing volleyball at the beach.
- Be more friendly and talk at night with American girls/boys.
- Invite people from different countries to come and visit my place.
- When I go shopping, have a chat with the clerk or other shoppers.
- Other: _____

TO REDUCE THE AMOUNT OF TIME I SPEAK MY NATIVE LANGUAGE

- Try as much as possible not to mix with people from the my country.
- Speak English with people from my country.
- Make an agreement to speak only English with people from the same country with a time limit. (Example: Every day after class for 1–2 hours we will speak only English.)
- Other: _____

TO SPEAK MORE ENGLISH AND LESS OF MY NATIVE LANGUAGE

- Tell the teacher to give more speaking opportunities.
- The teacher can be more strict and tell us never to use our native language.
- It depends on me (it is my own responsibility/choice).
- The teacher should give more opportunities for learners to express our opinions and discuss ideas.
- We listen to the teacher more.
- Other: _____

TO INCREASE TV-WATCHING TIME

- Visit friends or neighbors to watch TV.
- Watch the news for a few minutes every day (30 minutes?).
- Limit the amount of time spent on watching entertainment programs and watch more current events.
- Go to the movies more.
- Other: _____

TO INCREASE READING IN ENGLISH

- Read local free periodicals.
- Read children's books.
- Read *Sesame Street Wordbook*.
- Read the comic strips in the newspapers.
- Read bank statements, advertisements, and junk mail.
- Have a pen friend (write and read English).
- Before sleeping, read a little bit.
- Read out loud at home.
- Make reading into a habit (a certain amount of time every day).
- Other: _____

TO STUDY

- Make it into a habit.
- Prepare and review every day for a short time.
- Give yourself a reward (a cookie? a beer?) after you finish studying.
- Other: _____

COMMENTS

Worksheet 3

Writing a Learner Contract

Name: _____ Date: _____

Using the information you have written on Worksheet 1, Self-Monitoring Your Language Use, write at least two strengths in your study habits (two things that you do not want to change).

Write at least three habits that you want to change about your language use. For each one, write what you are going to do to change it. Use the list you and your classmates have generated for possible ways to increase or reduce the time you spend on a particular activity.

Assessing Your Speaking Skills

Aims: Practice oral tests in a nonthreatening environment; learn the various aspects of marking an oral test; think about what is important in oral production

Task Time: 15–30 minutes

Preparation Time: Several hours

Resources: Oral Test Pack, worksheet, Oral Test Mark Sheet, Oral Test Guidelines Check Sheet

PREAMBLE

Many learners feel that their speaking skills are inadequate and fear being tested on their oral ability. One way to give learners more confidence in their speaking skills is to allow them to "test" each other in a nonthreatening situation.

WHAT THE TEACHER HAS TO DO

1. Prepare an Oral Test Pack. This should include a variety of material to stimulate the learners to talk: pictures, diagrams, maps, prompt words.
2. Prepare a simple mark sheet to be used by the learners in the test.
3. Prepare an Oral Test Guidelines Check Sheet.
4. Group the items in Steps 1–3 into a folder with the worksheet.

CONTRIBUTOR: Lindsay Miller is an Assistant Professor in the English Department at the City University of Hong Kong.

WORKSHEET

ORAL TEST

Work with a partner. Collect an Oral Test Pack from the Test Section in the self-access center. In the Test Pack you will find:

1. Material to talk about
2. An Oral Test Mark Sheet
3. An Oral Test Guidelines Check Sheet

Stage 1

Decide who is the tester and who will be tested.

Stage 2

Sit together and use the material in the pack to perform an oral test. You may conduct the test in whatever way you want. Your test should last from 10 to 15 minutes. You may want to record the test.

Stage 3

Both the tester and the person who was tested should take a copy of the mark sheet and grade the oral performance. Do this independently; then compare your answers.

If there is some disagreement, discuss why you awarded the grade you did. Try to reach some agreement on a final grade.

Stage 4

Look at the Oral Test Guidelines Check Sheet and interpret your grade. Do you think the interpretation reflects your ability as a speaker of English?
Record your grade in your Independent Learning Diary.

Further Suggestion

Try a similar test again next month with a different partner. See if you can improve on the grade you have.

Sample Prompt Words for Oral Test

Choose some of the following topics to talk about during the oral test:

Family	Education	Home life
Sports	Hobbies	Likes/dislikes
Films	Holidays	Current events

ORAL TEST MARK SHEET

Circle the number you think is most appropriate in each category.

Language area	1 = poor	2 = fair	3 = good	4 = excellent
Fluency	1	2	3	4
Pronunciation	1	2	3	4
Grammar	1	2	3	4
Vocabulary	1	2	3	4
Communication	1	2	3	4
Overall performance	1	2	3	4

Comments:

ORAL TEST GUIDELINES CHECK SHEET

Look at the grade you and your partner have decided on for your oral test. Check it against the descriptions below:

Score = 20–24: You are a very good speaker of English. You can describe and explain pictures/diagrams with no hesitations and with sophisticated vocabulary. You may have a slight accent.

Score = 16–19: You are a good speaker of English. You can communicate easily and get your message across. Your language is mostly accurate but has some minor problems. You have some pronunciation problems with an obvious nonnative accent.

Score = 10–15: Your speaking skills are OK but need improving. You can explain the main points of a picture/diagram, but you make quite a lot of errors and sometimes you are not clear in your explanation. Your pronunciation often affects your communication.

Score = 6–9: Your speaking skills are quite weak. It takes you a long time to describe a picture/diagram. Your speaking lacks clarity and contains a lot of inaccurate grammar. Your pronunciation is poor and affects your communication.

Identifying Reading Strategies

Aims: Reflect on different first language reading strategies to develop for use in the target language

Task Time: Variable

Preparation Time: Variable

Resources: Worksheet

PREAMBLE

This task helps learners transfer the reading strategies they have in their first language to a foreign language. By comparing their own strategies to those of classmates, they will gain awareness of the different reading strategies they should try to develop. Some of the reading strategies learners most commonly need to acquire are (a) learning to guess and read for gist, even in their first language; (b) transferring reading strategies from the first to the second language; (c) using a dictionary to check on a meaning they have tentatively inferred; (d) skipping unfamiliar words and spending more time with the text than with the dictionary; and (e) choosing the most appropriate meaning of a word for the particular context.

WHAT THE TEACHER HAS TO DO

1. Prepare a worksheet for your learners similar to the example. Distribute the worksheet in class.
2. Ask your learners to complete the worksheet at home.
3. If desired, ask the learners to complete the optional Stage 3 in class.

VARIATION

Use the worksheet again after a certain time span to encourage learners to assess their own progress and to implement effective reading strategies.

CONTRIBUTOR: Carmen F. Santás is a teacher in the secondary school Antón Fraguas de Fontiñas and a teacher trainer in the Institute of Education of the University of Santiago de Compostela, Spain.

WORKSHEET

This questionnaire is about you as a reader during the current academic year. Write your answers on a sheet of paper. If it is difficult to answer in English, you can do so in your first language.

Name: _____ Date: _____

STAGE 1

These five questions are about you as a reader in your first language.

1. Apart from the books you had to read for school, how many books in your first language did you read voluntarily and why?
2. When you came across an unknown word, what did you usually do?

Self-Assessment

3. Did you ever read a passage that you couldn't understand even though you understood all the words? What was the cause of that lack of understanding?

4. Do you have any problems as a reader? What have you done about them?

5. Do you think you are an efficient reader? Why?

STAGE 2

The following questions are about you as a reader in English.

1. Did you read any simplified books in English? Tell how many you had to read and how many you read voluntarily.

2. Do you think that reading has helped you improve your English? How?

3. When you could not understand a passage, what was the reason? The amount of new vocabulary? Its syntactic structure? Its unfamiliar sociocultural meaning? Explain.

4. Whenever you were asked to read a simplified book in English, what purpose did the teacher(s) have in mind? Choose the three options that explain your case best.

   - Improve your communicative competence
   - Enlarge your vocabulary
   - Review grammatical structures
   - Make you familiar with syntactic structures that are different from the ones in your first language
   - Widen your knowledge of the world
   - Increase your autonomy as a learner
   - Give you something to do and enjoy in your free time
   - Get specific knowledge on a new subject
   - Others: explain.

5. When you read voluntarily, both in English and in your first language, why do you do it? Would you like to read more in English? Why?

STAGE 3

Compare your answers with those of your classmates. Get into groups of four or five with those whose answers are basically similar to yours. Write down the reasons the group has to read in English.

Identifying Your Grammar Problems

- [ ] beginner
- [ ] low intermediate
- [x] intermediate
- [ ] advanced

- [x] individual
- [ ] pair
- [ ] group
- [ ] tutor-assisted

- [ ] in class
- [x] out of class
- [ ] self-access center

Aims: Conduct a simple grammar self-analysis

Task Time: 1 hour

Preparation Time: 30 minutes

Resources: Sample of the learner's written work, worksheet, Grammar Errors Table, Grammar Errors Record Grid

PREAMBLE

Learners frequently complain that they have problems with grammar. It is revealing for them to examine and categorize their own errors before they plan for themselves a remedial program that fulfills their personal needs.

WHAT THE TEACHER HAS TO DO

1. Adapt the worksheet, table, and grid to suit your learners.
2. Advise the learners on how to use the worksheet: Go over the examples in class or ask the learners to use their dictionaries to discover what the grammatical names mean if they do not already know them.

VARIATION

Create worksheets for different levels of learners by making the examples simpler or more complex.

CONTRIBUTOR: Mabel C. P. Wong is a freelance ESL specialist in Victoria, Australia.

WORKSHEET

PREPARATION

You need a sample of your own writing that has been marked by a teacher.

BEFORE YOU BEGIN

Do you have problems identifying your own grammar problems? This worksheet is designed for learners who wish to improve their English grammar but have no idea what specific grammar problems they have. You will do an error analysis for yourself.

ACTIVITY 1

Look through all the errors in your sample work. To find out the grammatical name for each of your errors (if they are grammatical), use the Grammar Errors Table attached to this worksheet.

ACTIVITY 2

After identifying the grammatical names of your own mistakes, categorize them according to their nature (i.e., *misuse, omission, addition, incorrect form, word order*). Use the Grammar Errors Record Grid attached to this worksheet to record each error by putting a tick in the appropriate box according to error type and category. The tally will show you the frequency with which individual categories of errors occur.

ACTIVITY 3

The next step is to see which area(s) deserve(s) immediate attention. Generally speaking, two types of errors deserve urgent treatment:

1. High-frequency errors (i.e., errors that often happen)
2. Errors affecting communication or having irritating effects

Prioritize the grammatical points that you want to improve and locate relevant materials that will help you, or ask your tutor for assistance. Repeat this analysis from time to time to check on your progress.

GRAMMAR ERRORS TABLE

Example of grammar point	Grammatical name
a *happy* mother with a *healthy* baby.	Adjective
She was breathing *quietly* and *evenly*	Adverb
Dogs like to eat far more meat than human beings do.	Agreement
The car became an increasing necessity of life in the twentieth century. *A* car became an increasing necessity of life in the twentieth century.	Article
She *is* going to town. It must *have* been eaten.	Auxiliary verb
My brother is *younger than* me. Last year, terrorist activities were *worse than* in any of the previous twelve years.	Comparative
If I marry your sister, *we shall need* money to live on. *If I could afford* it, *I would buy* a boat.	Conditional
I washed the dishes, *and* I dried them. Peter is poor, *but* he is happy.	Connective
I *shall* do what you suggested. *Wouldn't* you like to come with me?	Modal verb
It is *impossible* to park the car *anywhere*. I knew I *wasn't* learning *anything whatsoever*.	Negation
He was a worried old *man*. Their *act* is out of date.	Noun

Example of grammar point	Grammatical name
We'll have to *hang around* for a while.	Phrasal verb
A plane has just *taken off*.	
The elderly man *in* the raincoat looks ill.	Preposition
It is unpleasant to work *with* that man.	
Send *us* a letter so we'll know where you are.	Pronoun
All the girls think *he*'s great, don't *they*?	
Only *a few of* the injured were saved.	Quantity
Your report contained large *numbers of* inaccuracies.	
When would you be coming down?	Question
I wonder *if you could tell me something about the book.*	
She *works* hard. She *worked* hard. She *has been working* hard.	Tense
She *spoke* to me. I *have cut* myself.	Verb

GRAMMAR ERRORS RECORD GRID

Key: 1 = Misuse, 2 = Omission, 3 = Addition, 4 = Incorrect form, 5 = Word order

Error category	1	2	3	4	5
Adjectives					
Adverbs					
Agreement					
Articles					
Auxiliary verbs					
Comparative					
Conditionals					
Connectives					
Modal verbs					
Negation					
Nouns					
Prepositions					
Pronouns					
Punctuation					

Self-Assessment

Error category	1	2	3	4	5
Quantity					
Questions					
Sentence patterns					
Tenses					
Verbs					

ALSO AVAILABLE FROM TESOL

Books for a Small Planet:
An Intercultural Bibliography for Young English Language Learners
Dorothy S. Brown

Diversity as Resource:
Redefining Cultural Literacy
Denise E. Murray, Editor

E-Mail for English Teaching:
Bringing the Internet and Computer Learning Networks
Into the Language Classroom
Mark Warschauer

More Than a Native Speaker:
An Introduction for Volunteers Teaching Abroad
Don Snow

New Ways in Teacher Education
Donald Freeman, with Steve Cornwell, Editors

New Ways in Teaching Grammar
Martha C. Pennington, Editor

New Ways in Teaching Listening
David Nunan and Lindsay Miller, Editors

New Ways in Teaching Reading
Richard R. Day, Editor

New Ways in Teaching Speaking
Kathleen M. Bailey and Lance Savage, Editors

New Ways in Teaching Vocabulary
Paul Nation, Editor

New Ways in Teaching Writing
Ronald V. White, Editor

New Ways in Teaching Young Children
Linda Schinke-Llano and Rebecca Rauff, Editors

For more information, contact

Teachers of English to Speakers of Other Languages, Inc.
1600 Cameron Street, Suite 300
Alexandria, Virginia 22314 USA
Tel. 703-836-0774 • Fax 703-836-7864
e-mail publ@tesol.edu